Hossein Bidgoli

INFORMATION SYSTEMS LITERACY AND SOFTWARE PRODUCTIVITY TOOLS

WordPerfect 5.1

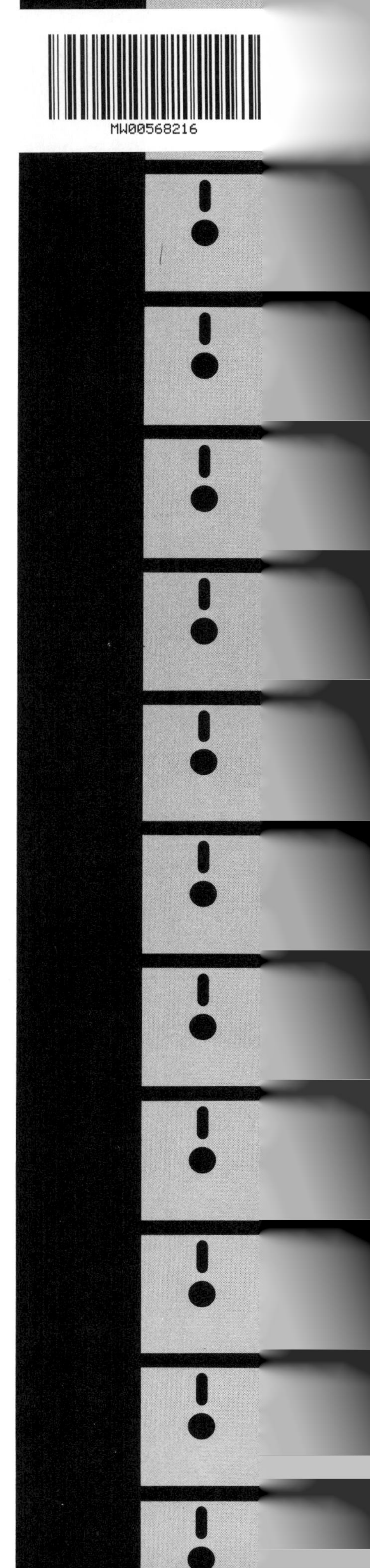

Macmillan Publishing Company
New York
Collier Macmillan Canada, Inc.
Toronto
Maxwell Macmillan International Publishing Group
New York Oxford Singapore Sydney

To so many fine memories of my brother, Mohsen, for his uncompromising belief in the power of education.

Cover photo by Jack McWilliams. The Walk-Through Computer is a permanent exhibit of The Computer Museum, Boston, MA.

Editor: Vernon R. Anthony
Production Editor: Rex Davidson
Art Coordinator: Ruth A. Kimpel
Photo Editor: Gail Meese
Text Designer: Anne Daly
Cover Designer: Russ Maselli
Production Buyer: Pamela D. Bennett

This book was set in Baskerville and Helvetica.

Printed in the United States of America

Macmillan Publishing Company
866 Third Avenue, New York, New York 10022

Collier Macmillan Canada, Inc.

Library of Congress Cataloging-in-Publication Data
Bidgoli, Hossein.
Information systems literacy and software productivity tools/Hossein Bidgoli.
p. cm.
Includes index.
Contents: bk. 1. Introductory concepts—bk. 2. DOS—bk. 3. WordPerfect 5.1—bk. 4. dBASE III PLUS—bk. 5. WordStar 5.5—bk. 6. Quattro—bk. 7. GoldSpread—bk. 8. IBM BASIC—bk. 9. DOS, WordPerfect 5.1, Lotus 1-2-3, and dBASE III PLUS—bk. 10. DOS, WordStar 5.5, Lotus 1-2-3, and dBASE III PLUS.
ISBN 0-02-309429-X (bk. 3.)
1. Electronic data processing. 2. Computer software. I. Title.
QA76.B488 1991 90-20366
005.369—dc20 CIP

Printing: 1 2 3 4 5 6 7 8 9 Year: 1 2 3 4

Preface

Information Systems Literacy and Software Productivity Tools: WordPerfect 5.1 is a component of a modular series of textbooks developed for use in introductory computing coursework. This WordPerfect text is written for first courses in word processing, or for use in conjunction with texts in any course where a word processing tutorial is required. While the text is written to WordPerfect 5.1, the Appendix discusses germane differences in earlier versions of the software.

The software tutorials in this book are designed to give the student comprehensive training and reference, all broken down into manageably sized chapters. This approach gives the instructor a choice as to which and how many topics to cover, and gives the student a valuable reference to use long after the class is completed. Advanced topics not covered in many texts are included here, as a growing number of students are coming into introductory courses with some software literacy; this book allows students to go further in their studies.

The software chapters are pedagogically designed with the student in mind. Features include:

- Introductory sections that explain, in basic terms, what the software is, why it was developed, and how it is used. Too many books "jump right in" without giving the student a sense of context.
- Numerous, real-life examples. This book teaches the use of commands by example so the command is clear and in context.
- Frequent use of computer screen illustrations to augment written instruction.
- Each chapter ends with 15–25 review questions, 5–8 hands-on experience assignments, and 10 multiple choice and 10 true/false questions.
- Each chapter includes a complete summary of key terms and key computer commands.
- When appropriate, chapters include a unique section entitled "Misconceptions and Solutions." Common errors, improper operating procedures, and how to avoid/solve them are highlighted for the student.

In any hands-on computer lab, having an accurate text makes managing the lab far easier. The best way to make a text accurate is to use it. In the four years that I took developing this text I have received corrections and suggestions that make this book one you should find both easy to use and reliable.

Command Summaries are included in appendices for all the software packages covered. Answers to selected review questions can be found in the appendices to assist the students in their studies. Also included is a guide to the use of the various student versions of the software covered.

The software modules for this text series are accompanied by a complete instructor's manual with lecture outlines, answers to review questions/exercises, and additional projects. Data diskettes with which students can access all the programs and exercises are included in this manual.

Acknowledgments

Several colleagues reviewed different versions of this manuscript and made constructive suggestions. Without their help the manuscript could not have been refined. The help and comments of the following reviewers are greatly appreciated: Kirk Arnett, Mississippi State University; Tom Berliner, University of Texas—Dallas; Glen Boswell, San Antonio College; Michael Davis, Texas Technical University; Steve Deam, Milwaukee Area Technical College; Beth Defoor, Eastern New Mexico University—Clovis, Richard Ernst, Sullivan Junior College; Barbara Felty, Harrisburg Area Community College; Pat Fenton, West Valley College; Phyllis Helms, Randolph Community College; Mehdi Khosrowpour, Pennsylvania State—Harrisburg; Candice Marble, Wentworth Military Academy; John Miller, Williamsport Area Community College; Charles McDonald, East Texas State University; Sylvia Meyer, Community College of Vermont; John Miller, Williamsport Area Community College; J. D. Oliver, Prairie View A&M University; Greg Pierce, Penn State University; Eugene Rathswohl, University of San Diego; Herbert Rebhun, University of Houston—Downtown; R. D. Shelton, Loyola College; Sandra Stalker, North Shore Community College; G. W. Willis, Baylor University; and Judy Yeager, Western Michigan University.

Many different groups assisted me in completing this project. I am grateful to over four thousand students who attended by executive seminars and various classes in information systems and software productivity tools. They helped me fine-tune the manuscript during its various stages. My friend Bahram Ahanin helped me to improve many concepts of hardware/software and put them in a non-technical and easy-to-understand format. My colleague and friend Dr. Reza Azarmsa provided support and encouragement. I am grateful for all of his encouragement. My colleague Andrew Prestage assisted me in numerous trouble-spots by running and debugging many of the screens presented in the book. My colleague Robert Grossberg tested the manuscript in several of his classes and assisted me in developing numerous test questions.

Several of my students assisted me in running and testing the accuracy of the screens presented throughout the book. I thank Daryl Dunn, Sandra Retzke, Wendy Kramme, Judy Buchanan, Catherine Begg, and Kathleen Whelan.

I am indebted to Jacki Lawson, who typed and retyped various versions of this manuscript. Her thoroughness and patience made it easier to complete this project. She deserves special recognition for all this work. David Koeth designed the majority of the charts presented in the first phase of the text development. His help and thoroughness is appreciated.

A team of professionals from Macmillan Publishing Company assisted me from the very beginning of this venture. Charles Stewart had faith in this project's potential from the onset, for which I thank him. The assistance of Vern Anthony, my executive editor, in guiding me throughout the project is greatly appreciated. Rex Davidson, Jo Anna Arnott, Gail Meese, Ruth Kimple, Teresa George, and Michelle Byron, all from Macmillan, assisted me in completing this project. I am grateful and appreciate their work.

Finally, I want to thank my family for their support and encouragement throughout my life. My two sisters, Azam and Akram, deserve my very special thanks and recognition.

Dr. Hossein Bidgoli is professor of Management Information Systems at California State University, Bakersfield. He holds a Ph.D. degree in systems science from Portland State University with a specialization in design and implementation of MIS. His master's degree is in MIS from Colorado State University. Dr. Bidgoli's background includes experience as a systems analyst, information systems consultant, financial analyst, and he was the director of the Microcomputer Center at Portland State University.

Dr. Bidgoli, a two-time winner of the MPPP (Meritorious Performance and Professional Promise) award for outstanding performance in teaching, research and university/community service is the author of fifteen texts and numerous professional papers and articles presented and published throughout the United States on the topics of computers and MIS. Dr. Bidgoli has also designed and implemented over twenty executive seminars on all aspects of information systems and decision support systems.

Contents

WORDPERFECT 5.1

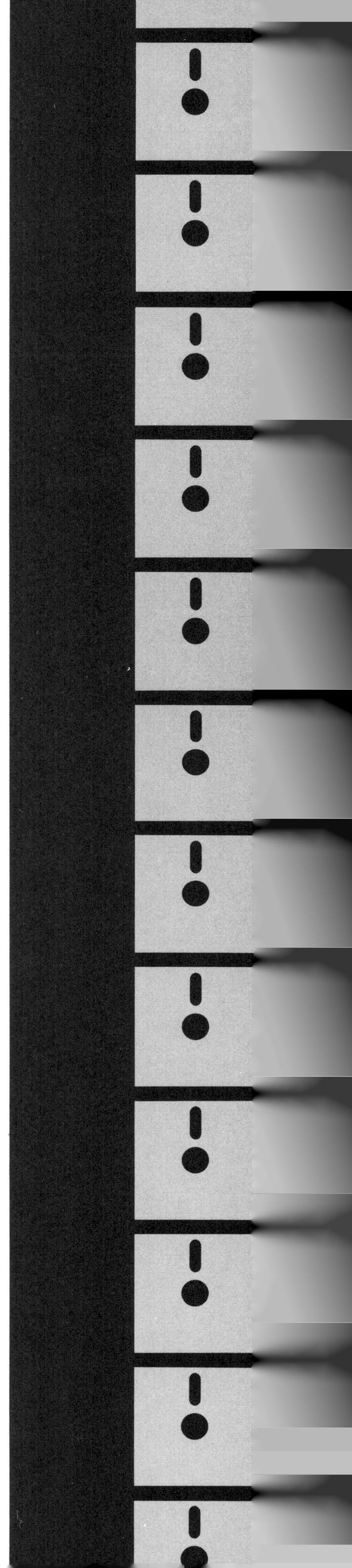

The World of Microcomputers

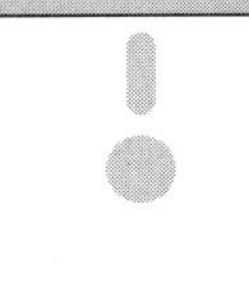
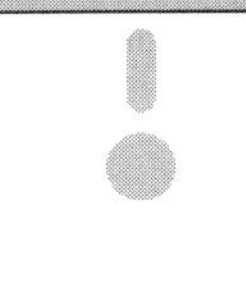

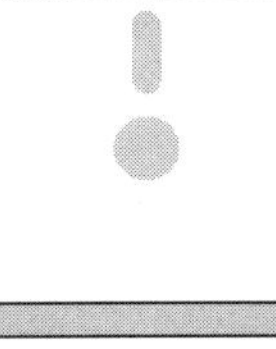

1

1–1 INTRODUCTION

In this chapter we discuss microcomputer fundamentals. Hardware and software for micros are explained, and different classes of application software are introduced. We present guidelines for successful selection and maintenance of microcomputers and we discuss the advantages of micros compared to mainframes. The chapter concludes with a hands-on session with a microcomputer.

1–2 DEFINING A MICROCOMPUTER

The terms personal computer, PC, micro, and **microcomputer** refer to the smallest type of computer when measured by such attributes as memory, cost, size, speed, and sophistication. Although small, the ever-increasing power and capability of personal computers sometimes blur the difference between PCs and larger computers.

Since the beginning of the microcomputer era in about 1975, the capability of these computers has improved beyond imagination. Still, some experts believe this is only the beginning and there is much more to be done by these computers.

A typical microcomputer consists of input, output, and memory devices. Figure 1–1 illustrates a typical microcomputer system. The **input device** is usually a keyboard. A PC keyboard is similar to a typewriter keyboard, with some additional keys. Figure 1–2 displays an IBM enhanced keyboard. Other input devices include the mouse, touch technology, light pens, graphics tablets, optical character readers (OCR), magnetic ink character recognition (MICR), cameras, sensors, and bar codes. In the future, there may be voice input devices as well.

The most common **output devices** for microcomputers are a monitor—sometimes called a CRT (cathode-ray tube) or VDT (video display terminal)—and a printer. The output generated on the monitor is called soft copy, and the printed output is referred to as hard copy. Other kinds of output devices include cameras and plotters.

There are two types of monitors. The majority of microcomputers use a monochrome screen. As the name indicates, this type of screen generates one

Figure 1–1
A Typical Microcomputer System. (Cobalt Productions/Macmillan).

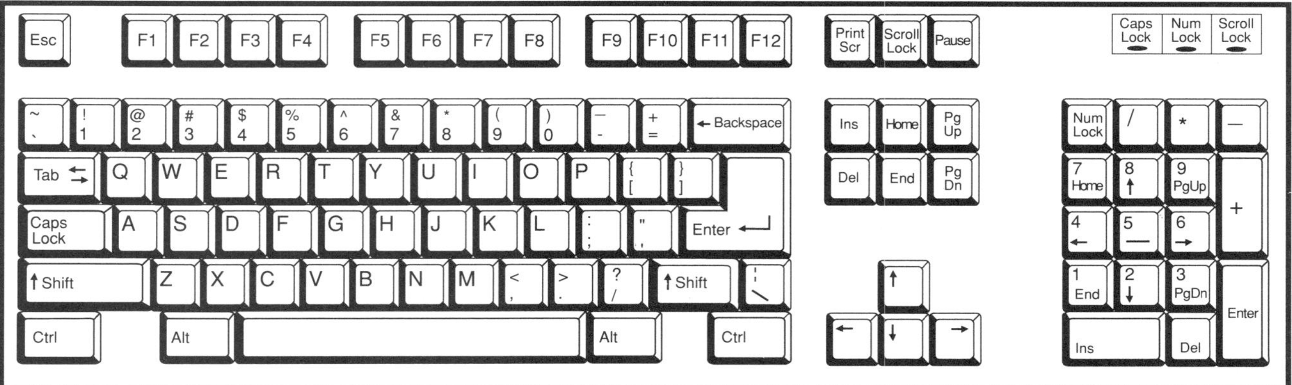

Figure 1–2
An IBM Enhanced Keyboard

color, such as green or amber. Monochrome monitors can generate graphics output if your computer is equipped with a graphics card or graphics adapter.

The other type of monitor is a color monitor—sometimes referred to as an RGB (red-green-blue) monitor. Color monitors come in several types: CGA, EGA, and VGA.

The sharpness of images on the display monitor is referred to as the resolution. The intersection of a row and a column is called a pixel; the greater the number of pixels, the higher the resolution. CGA, EGA, and VGA monitors present different resolutions. A CGA (Color Graphics Adapter) monitor displays 320 by 200 pixels in four colors.

An EGA (Enhanced Graphics Adapter) monitor displays 640 by 350 pixels in 16 colors. More advanced versions of EGA monitors can display 640 by 480 pixels in 16 colors and 320 by 200 pixels in 256 colors.

A VGA (Video Graphics Array) monitor can display 640 by 480 pixels in 16 colors and 320 by 200 pixels in 256 colors. The most recent graphics add-on board, this card was introduced in 1987 by the IBM PS/2 series computers.

Boards or cards are used to upgrade or expand the computer's capacities. These boards or cards perform many tasks. Some are used to expand memory, others are used as peripheral devices.

The processing part of a microcomputer is the CPU (central processing unit). Also called the microprocessor, the CPU includes three components. The main memory stores data, information, and instructions. The arithmetic logic unit (ALU) performs arithmetic and logical operations. Arithmetic operations include addition, subtraction, division, and multiplication. Logical operations include any types of comparisons, such as sorting (putting data into a particular order) or searching (choosing a particular data item). The control unit serves as the commander of the system. It tells the microcomputer what to do and how to do it. Figure 1–3 shows two different microprocessor chips or microchips.

1–3 MORE ON THE KEYBOARD

As you can see in figure 1–2, an enhanced keyboard is divided into three sections. Across the top are 12 function keys. Some keyboards have the function keys on the left. With most application software, these keys perform special functions, or they can be programmed to perform a particular task. For

A.

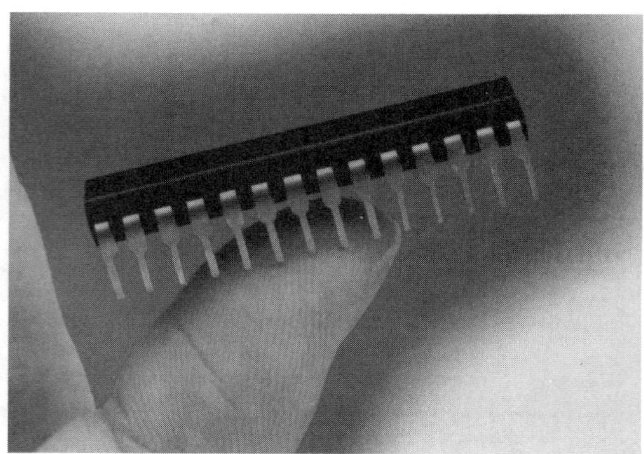

B.

Figure 1–3
A. The Motorola MC 68020 Microprocessor in the Protective Ceramic Package (Courtesy of Motorola, Inc.). B. A Microprocessor. (Courtesy of Radio Shack, A Division of Tandy Corporation).

example, Lotus 1-2-3, dBASE, and WordPerfect use function keys F1 through F10 for performing different tasks.

The middle part of the keyboard is similar to a typewriter keyboard. However, there are some special keys that a typewriter does not have—the Alt key and Ctrl keys, for example.

On the right side of the keyboard is a numeric keypad similar to that of an adding machine, used for cursor movement or, when the Num Lock key is pressed, to facilitate numeric data entry.

The purpose of function keys and some of the special keys varies in different application programs. For example, in WordPerfect, the F1 key performs undelete operations. In 1-2-3 or dBASE, it accesses on-line help.

1–4 OTHER NECESSARY DEVICES

Besides typical input/output devices, some additional devices are required for effective use of a microcomputer. These devices include disk drives and adapter cards.

1–4–1 Disk Drives

Disk drives are used to read and store data or information from and to a disk into the memory. Disk drives come in various capacities. You may have one or more floppy disk drives, and you also may have a **hard disk** drive. As you will read later, hard disks are capable of storing large quantities of information. The capacity of a hard disk is many times greater than a **floppy disk**. A floppy disk can hold from 360K (kilobytes) to 1.44M (megabytes) of information. The capacity of a hard disk varies from 5M to 300M or more.

The capacity of a storage device is measured in terms of bits or bytes. A bit (BInary digiT) is the smallest piece of information understood by a computer. A bit is either a 1 or a 0, indicating either an on or an off condition. A byte is a string of eight bits acting as a single piece of information. A byte is roughly equivalent to one character. For example, if you type "Susan" on your

Table 1–1

0 or 1 is equal to one bit
8 bits is equal to one byte
1,024 (2^{10}) bytes is equal to one kilobyte (K)
1,048,576 (2^{20}) bytes is equal to one megabyte (M)
1,073,741,824 (2^{30}) bytes is equal to one gigabyte
1,099,511,627,776 (2^{40}) bytes is equal to one terabyte

computer, it will occupy approximately five bytes of memory. Table 1–1 shows various memory equivalents.

1–4–2 Adapter Cards

Adapter cards are used to attach a particular option to the system unit. They are installed in expansion slots (channels) inside the system unit. Typical adapter cards may include the following:

- Disk drive card for connecting disk drives to the system unit
- Display card for connecting CRT to the system unit
- Memory card for connecting additional RAM to the existing memory
- Clock card for connecting a clock to the system unit
- Modem card for connecting a modem to your PC
- Printer interface card for connecting a printer to your computer

The original IBM PC has five expansion slots, the IBM XT and AT have eight slots. The adapter cards usually have outlet ports that are accessed at the back of the system unit. It is important to remember that the newer PCs do not require as many adapter cards. Ports are either parallel or serial and are used to connect devices to the system. You must connect a serial device to a serial port and a parallel device to a parallel port. Serial devices transfer one bit of data at a time, parallel devices transfer groups of bits at a time.

1–5 TYPES OF PRIMARY MEMORIES

There are two kinds of memory: main, or **primary memory,** and auxiliary, or secondary memory. Main memory is the heart of the microcomputer, usually referred to as **RAM** (Random-Access Memory). This is volatile memory—data stored in RAM are lost when you turn off your computer. To avoid this type of loss, you should always save your work on a storage device, such as a disk.

Three other types of memory also are referred to as main memory, but the user does not have direct control over them. These include:

- **ROM** (Read-Only Memory): A prefabricated chip supplied by vendors. This memory stores some general-purpose instructions or programs—DOS commands, for example.
- **PROM** (Programmable Read-Only Memory): By using a special device, the user can program this memory. However, once programmed, the user cannot erase this type of memory.

- **EPROM** (Erasable Programmable Read-Only Memory): This type of read-only memory can be programmed by the user and, as the name indicates, erased and programmed again.

1–6 TYPES OF SECONDARY MEMORIES

Because the main memory of a microcomputer is limited, expensive, and volatile, secondary storage devices are used for mass data storage. **Secondary memory** is nonvolatile, and can be broadly classified into magnetic and optical.

1–6–1 Magnetic Storage Devices

Magnetic storage devices include floppy disks, mini-floppy disks, hard disks, and the Bernoulli Box. The capacity of a floppy or hard disk depends on its technical features. There are three types of standard disks: 3-½ inches, 5-¼ inches, and 8 inches. The most recent floppy just entering into the market is a 2-inch floppy.

Disks can be single-density, double density, or high-density. Density refers to the amount of information that can be stored on a disk. They can also be single-sided or double-sided. A 5-¼ inch, single-sided, single-density floppy can hold roughly 125K; a 5-¼ inch, single-sided, double-density floppy can hold about 250K; a 5-¼ inch, double-sided, double-density floppy can hold approximately 360K; and a high-density disk (sometimes called quad-density) can hold up to 1.2M. A 3-½ inch floppy disk can store 720K per side, or 1.44M on a double-sided disk.

A hard disk (sometimes called a Winchester disk) can be either 14, 8, 5-¼, or less than 4 inches in diameter. The capacity of these devices varies from 5 megabytes to 1 gigabyte.

A Bernoulli Box is a removable medium. This means after finishing your computer work you can pull this device out and store it in a safe location. This is not possible with a hard disk. A Bernoulli Box uses high-capacity floppy disks to store 10M or more of information. Generally speaking, it is less damage-prone than a hard disk, because the Bernoulli Box drive head, which records the data, does not move as a hard disk drive head does. In a Bernoulli Box the floppy disk moves toward the stationary read/write head. Figure 1–4 shows a Bernoulli Box.

Figure 1–4
A Bernoulli Box (Cobalt Productions/Macmillan)

Currently, the most commonly used secondary storage device is the 3-½ inch floppy disk. However, at the beginning of the PC era 5-¼ inch floppy disks were the most commonly used secondary storage devices. A 5-¼ inch disk is enclosed in a permanent vinyl jacket to protect the disk. A floppy disk is made of plastic material coated with magnetic material. After using a floppy disk you should put it back in its paper cover to protect it against dirt and dust. Don't put your fingers on exposed portions of the disk or data loss may result. Figure 1–5 highlights important areas of a 5-¼ inch disk.

Optical Technologies 1–6–2

Three types of optical storage have attracted much attention in recent years: CD ROM, WORM, and erasable optical disk. The advantages of optical technology devices are their durability and storage capacity. The major drawback of optical technology is its slow speed. However, the speed problem is being resolved gradually.

As the name indicates, **CD ROM** (compact disk read-only memory) is a permanent device. Information is recorded by disk-mastering machines. A CD ROM is similar to an audio compact disk. It can be duplicated and distributed throughout the organization. Its major application is for large permanent databases; for example, public-domain databases such as libraries, real estate information, and corporate financial information.

WORM (Write Once, Read Many) also is a permanent device. Information can be recorded once and cannot be altered. Its major drawback compared

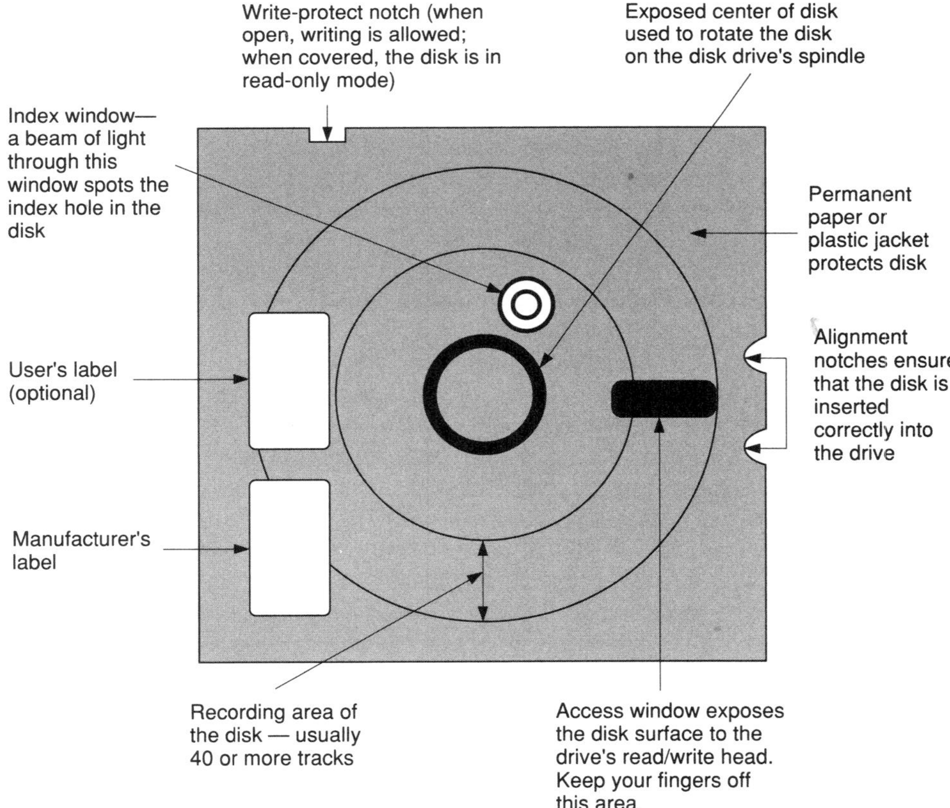

Figure 1–5
A 5-¼ Inch Floppy Disk

Figure 1–6
Optical Storage Devices for Microcomputers

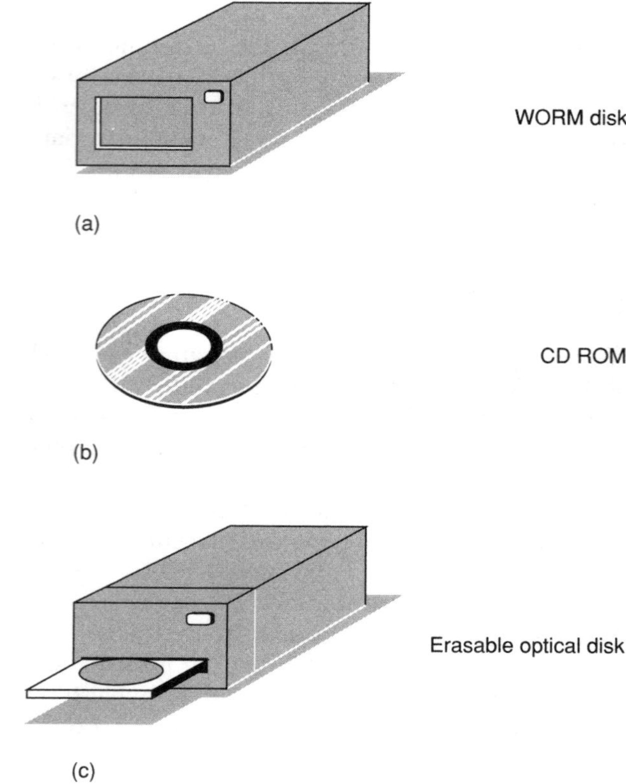

to CD ROM is that you cannot duplicate the disk. You use a WORM for storing information that must be kept permanently; for example, information related to annual reports, nuclear power plants, airports, and railroads.

An **erasable optical disk** is used when high-volume storage and updating are essential. The information can be recorded and erased repeatedly. Figure 1–6 shows these different technologies.

1–7 MEMORY CAPACITY AND PROCESSOR SPEED

Microcomputer RAM capacity usually starts at 256K, but most vendors now offer 512K or 640K PCs. PCs with capacities of 1 to 4 megabytes are becoming more common and, in the future, will approach minicomputer capacity.

When you purchase a computer, you should calculate the memory requirements for your computing needs. Although you may have a PC with 640K of RAM, all of it is not accessible to you. A large portion of this memory is used by the application software. As an example, Lotus 1-2-3 Release 2.01 uses almost 200K of RAM. So in a 640K PC, you are left with only 440K of user memory.

Another consideration regarding your computer is speed. The speed of the processor is measured in megahertz (MHz) and usually varies from 4 MHz to 33 MHz. Soon, speeds of 50 MHz or more may be available. The higher the processor speed, the faster the computer.

A factor that has direct effect on speed is the word size of the processor. Word size indicates the number of characters that can be processed simultaneously. Word size varies from 8 to 32 bits for microcomputers. The bigger the word size, the faster the computer. The speed of your microcomputer may have a direct effect on your business operation. With a faster computer you can process more information in a shorter period of time. However, you should consider the additional cost incurred by buying the more powerful PCs and the marginal benefit to be gained.

1–8 GENERAL CAPABILITIES OF MICROCOMPUTER SOFTWARE

A microcomputer can perform a variety of tasks by using either commercial software or software developed in-house. In-house developed software is usually more expensive than commercial software. However, this software is customized and should better fit your needs. Thousands of software programs are available for PCs. The following are typical commercial programs and applications available for microcomputers.

1–8–1 Word Processing Software

A microcomputer used as a **word processor** is similar to a typewriter with a memory. With a word processor, you can generate documents, make deletions and insertions, and cut and paste. Word processing programs are becoming more sophisticated, and some of these programs provide limited graphics and data management features.

There are many word processing programs on the market. Some of the most popular ones are Multimate from Ashton-Tate, Officewriter from Office Solutions, WordPerfect from WordPerfect Corp., WordStar from WordStar International, PC-Write from Quicksoft, Word from Microsoft, and Volkswriter from Lifetree Software, Inc.

1–8–2 Spreadsheet Software

A spreadsheet is simply a table of rows and columns. **Spreadsheet software** can be broadly classified into two types.

The first type is a dedicated spreadsheet. This means that the program performs only spreadsheet analysis. VisiCalc (by Visicorp) is a good example. The other type of spreadsheet package is integrated software, which means it can perform more than one type of analysis. You can use 1-2-3, for example, to perform spreadsheet analysis as well as maintaining a database and doing graphics. Some experts believe 1-2-3 is not a truly integrated package because it does not offer word processing and communication. However, although this is true, 1-2-3 can easily use these features from other software.

Other popular integrated packages include Electronic Desk from the Software Group, Inc., Framework from Ashton-Tate, Smart Software System from Innovative Software, Inc., Symphony from Lotus Development Corporation, UniCalc from Lattice, Inc., Excel from Microsoft, SuperCalc 5.0 from Computer Associates International, Inc., and Quattro from Borland International.

The number of jobs that can be performed by a spreadsheet program is unlimited. Generally speaking, any application suitable for a row and column analysis is a candidate for a typical spreadsheet. For example, you can use a spreadsheet to prepare a budget, and then, manipulating variables, the spreadsheet can perform some impressive "what-if" analysis. You could reduce your predicted income by 2 percent and ask the spreadsheet to calculate the effect of this change on other items in the spreadsheet.

1–8–3 Database Software

Database software is designed to perform database operations such as file creation, deletion, modification, search, sort, merge, and join (combining two files based on a common key). A **file** is a collection of records, a record is a collection of fields, and a field is a collection of characters.

Popular database programs include Business Filevision from Telos Software Products, dBASE III PLUS and IV from Ashton-Tate, PC-File III from Buttonware, Inc., Q&A from Symantec, Paradox from Ansa Software, Omnis Quartz from Blyth Software, DataEase from DataEase International, FoxBase and FoxPro from Fox Software, and R-Base from Microrim Corporation.

A database also can be compared to a table of rows and columns. The rows correspond to a record, and the columns correspond to the fields within the record. Two common applications of a database are sorting and searching records. In sort operations, the operator enters a series of records in any order then asks the database management program to sort the records in ascending or descending order, based on the data in the fields. Search operations are even more interesting. You can search for data items that meet certain criteria. You can, for example, search for all the MIS students who have GPAs greater than 3.6 and who are under 20 years of age. Some databases (such as Q&A) allow you to search for key words within a text file.

1–8–4 Graphics Software

Graphics software is designed to present data in graphic format. With this software, data can be converted into a line graph to show a trend, to a pie chart to highlight the components of a data item, and to other types of graphs for various analyses. Masses of data can be converted to a graph and, in a glance, you can discover the general pattern of the data. Graphs can highlight patterns and correlation of data items. They also make data presentation a more manageable job. Integrated packages such as 1-2-3 or Symphony have graphics capabilities, or you can use a dedicated graphics package.

Three popular graphics packages are Energraphics from Enertronics Research, Inc., Harvard Graphics from Software Publishing Corporation, and Freelance from Lotus Development Corporation.

1–8–5 Communications Software

Using a modem and **communications software,** your microcomputer can connect you to a wealth of information available in public and private databases. Several executives can simultaneously work on the same report in several different states or countries by using communications software. The report is sent back and forth to each location until it is completed. With communications software and a modem, remote job entry becomes an easy task. A modem converts computer signals (digital signals) to signals that can be transferred on a telephone line (analog signals).

Some programs, such as Symphony, include a communications program within the package itself. However, there are many other communications software products on the market, among them Crosstalk from Microstuf, Inc., On-Line from Micro-Systems Software, Inc., PFS: Access from Software Publishing Corp., and Smartcom II from Hayes Microcomputer Products, Inc.

Desktop Publishing Software 1–8–6

Desktop publishing software is used to produce professional-quality documents (with or without graphics) using relatively inexpensive hardware and software. All that is needed is a PC, a desktop publishing software package, and a letter-quality or laser printer. Desktop publishing has evolved as a result of three major factors: inexpensive PCs, inexpensive laser printers, and sophisticated and easy-to-use software.

Desktop publishing enables you to produce high quality screen output, and then transfer it to the printer in a "what you see is what you get" (WYSIWYG) environment. You can use desktop publishing for creating newsletters, brochures, training manuals, transparencies, posters, and books (see fig. 1–7).

A.

B.

Figure 1–7
A. Desktop Publishing Combines Text, Graphics, and Illustrations (Courtesy of Hewlett-Packard).
B. With Desktop Publishing, Business Professionals Can Prepare High Quality Documents (Courtesy of Hewlett-Packard)

There are several desktop publishing software packages available. Pagemaker from Aldus and Ventura Publisher from Xerox Corporation are two of the most popular ones.

1–8–7 Financial Planning Software

Financial planning software works with large amounts of data and performs diverse financial analyses. These analyses include present value, future value, rate of return, cash flow, depreciation, and budgeting.

Some popular programs for financial planning are DTFPS from Desk Top Financial Solutions, Inc., Excel from Microsoft Corp., Finar from Finar Research Systems, Ltd., Javelin from Javelin Software Corp., Micro-DSS/Finance from Addison-Wesley Publishing Co., 1-2-3 from Lotus Development Corporation, IFPS from Execucom Systems, and Micro Plan from Chase Laboratories, Inc.

With these programs, you can plan and analyze your financial situation. For example, you can calculate how much your $2,000 IRA will be at 10 percent interest in 30 years, or you can discount all future cash flows into today's dollar. You can figure out how much you have to deposit in the bank in order to save $60,000 in 10 years for your child's education.

1–8–8 Accounting Software

Aside from spreadsheet software, which has widespread applications in the accounting field, there are many dedicated **accounting programs** that are able to perform accounting tasks. The tasks performed by these programs include general ledgers, account receivables, account payables, payrolls, balance sheets, and income statements. Depending on the price, these programs vary in sophistication.

Some of the more popular accounting programs are One Write Plus from Gerat American Software, Business Works PC from Manzanita Software Systems, 4-in-1 Basic Accounting from Real World Corp., Peachtree from Peachtree Software, Inc., and DacEasy Accounting from Dac Software, Inc.

1–8–9 Project-Management Software

A project consists of a series of related activities. Building a house, designing an order-entry system, or writing a thesis are examples of projects. The goal of **project-management software** is to help decision-makers keep the time and budget under control by resolving scheduling problems. Project-management software helps managers to plan and set achievable goals. It also highlights the bottlenecks and the relationships among different activities. These programs enable you to study the cost, time, and resource effect of any change in the schedule.

Popular project-management programs include Harvard Total Project Manager from Software Publishing Corp., Micro Planner 6 from Micro Planning International, Microsoft Project from Microsoft Corp., Superproject Expert from Computer Associates, and Time Line from Symantec.

1–8–10 Computer-Aided Design (CAD) Software

Computer-aided design (CAD) software is used for drafting and design. CAD has replaced the traditional tools of drafting and design such as T-square, triangle, paper, and pencil, and it is being used extensively in the architectural and engineering industries. CAD software does not belong only to the large corporations any more. With the new 286-, 386-, and 486-based PCs and significant price reduction, small companies and individuals can afford this software. Because the new PCs have larger memory and are significantly faster than earlier PCs, they are able to take advantage of the majority of features offered by CAD programs.

There are several CAD programs on the market including AutoCAD from Autodesk, Cadkey from Cadkey, and VersaCAD from VersaCAD (see fig. 1–8).

1–9 GUIDELINES FOR SELECTING A MICROCOMPUTER

There are many kinds of microcomputers on the market, making the selection task a difficult one. In this section and the next, we provide you with some general guidelines regarding the purchase and maintenance of a microcomputer. These guidelines will help you choose a suitable computer and maintain it more easily.

A.

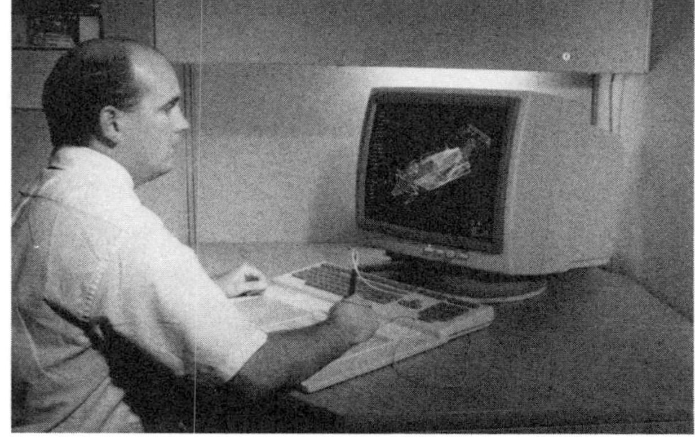

B.

Figure 1–8
A. A CAD System for Detailed Architectural Design (Larry Hamill/Macmillan). B. A CAD System for Design of a Multi-component Product (Larry Hamill/Macmillan). C. A CAD System of an Indy Car Rear Wing (Larry Hamill/Macmillan)

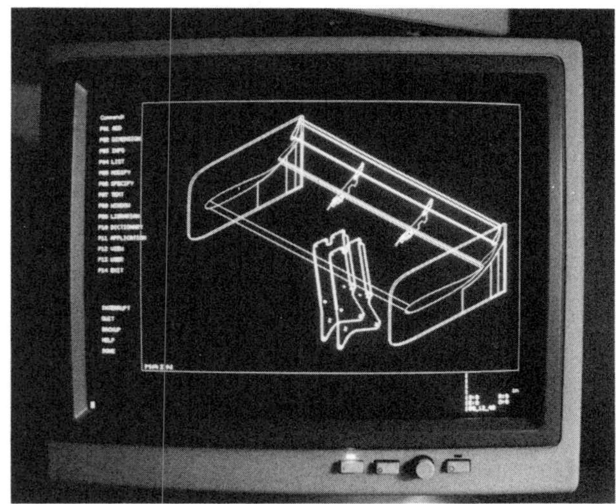

C.

Before you start looking, you should define your requirements. Sometimes this is called the "wish list" approach. When you are ready to buy, you should have a clear idea of the microcomputer you need and the specific applications you want it to handle. Remember, if you need a particular kind of software, you must have the hardware to run it.

After defining your software and hardware needs, you should look at technical support and vendor reputation. Important factors regarding selection and maintenance of a microcomputer follow.

Good software should:

- be easy to use
- be able to handle your business volume
- have good documentation
- have training available
- have updates available (free of charge or for a minimum charge)
- have local support
- come from a reputable vendor
- have a low cost

Good hardware should:

- have a comfortable keyboard
- have function keys
- have a general operating system (OS/2, MS-DOS, PC-DOS, or UNIX)
- have 16-bit or bigger processor (word) size
- be expandable (memory and peripheral)
- have adequate channel capacity or expansion slots
- have a low cost

A good monitor should:

- be separated from the system unit (not be built-in)
- be easy to read
- have a standard number of characters per row and column (80 columns by 25 rows)

A good disk drive should:

- have a built-in, not separate, disk drive
- have adequate storage capacity
- have a hard disk option

A good printer should:

- have a standard printer interface (without additional devices)
- produce quality output
- have high speed

- have a reasonable amount of noise suppression
- let you change tape, ribbons, or toner cartridge easily
- have a low cost

A good vendor should:

- have a good reputation
- have a knowledgeable staff
- have training available for hardware and software
- have a hot line available
- support newsletters and user groups
- provide a "loaner" in case of break down
- provide updates (trade-in options)

A good contract should:

- have a warranty period
- state a flexible time for repair
- limit down time and inconvenience by providing flexible repair visits and timely repair of the computer
- have reasonable terms for contract renewal
- allow relocation or reassignment of the present contract
- observe confidentiality issues

1–10 TAKING CARE OF YOUR MICROCOMPUTER

To maintain the health of your microcomputer you should follow these guidelines:

- Protect your microcomputer against dirt, dust, and smoke.
- Make backups and keep your backups in different locations.
- Avoid any kind of liquid spills.
- Maintain steady power. Use surge protectors and lightning arresters.
- Protect the machine from static by using humidifiers or antistatic spray devices.
- Do not use a disk that you are not familiar with (to avoid computer viruses—the deadly programs that can corrupt data).
- Don't download information to your computer from unknown bulletin boards. (Downloading means importing information from other computers by using a telephone line.)
- Acquire insurance for your computer equipment.

1–11 ADVANTAGES OF MICROCOMPUTERS

Generally speaking, a microcomputer offers several advantages compared to a mainframe computer. With extended memory and increased speed, microcomputers can perform on a smaller scale many of the tasks performed by a mainframe. We can summarize the advantages of microcomputers compared with mainframes as follows:

- They are easier to use.
- They are less threatening to non-computer experts.
- The user has more control.
- They are relatively inexpensive.
- They can be portable.

1–12 YOU AND YOUR PC: A HANDS-ON SESSION

If the disk operating system (DOS) is in drive A (the top disk drive, or the left disk drive, in a two-drive system), when you turn the computer on, your microcomputer will ask for the date. Most IBM or IBM-compatible computers come with a DOS disk. Either type the date in the desired format or press Enter to skip this prompt. The computer then asks you for the time. Either type the time in the desired format or press Enter. Now you are at the A> prompt. Figure 1–9 shows how your screen looks during the getting-started procedure.

If your computer has a hard disk this procedure is slightly different. You will start the system from the hard disk, and your prompt will be C> instead of A>. From the prompt, or disk operating system mode, you can go to any application software. For example, pull the DOS disk out of the drive, insert the Lotus System disk, type 123, and press Enter to load 1-2-3 into RAM.

When you are at the A> prompt, you are in RAM. We call this area a working or temporary area. This means any work in this area will disappear if you turn the computer off. To make your work permanent, you must transfer it to a **permanent area**. Any application program provides you with some type of save or copy command for transferring your work from RAM to disk. The permanent area can be either floppy disk, hard disk, or cassette. Your work stays in the permanent area until you erase it.

Beginning computer users are always worried about making mistakes. What happens if you make a mistake? Don't panic. Your mistakes easily can be corrected. Some computers and application programs have an UNDO command. In the worst case, you can correct your mistake by typing over your previous material. Remember, any address or cell in the computer memory can hold only one value at a time. As soon as you type a new value, the old one disappears.

Figure 1–9
Starting the System

```
Current date is Tue 1-01-80
Enter new date (mm-dd-yy): 1-1-91
Current time is 0:00:52.89
Enter new time: 15:25


Microsoft(R) MS-DOS(R)  Version 3.30
                (C)Copyright Microsoft Corp 1981-1987



A>
```

1–13 DEFINING A COMPUTER FILE

A computer file is basically an electronic document. One way to create a document is to enter it using the keyboard. As soon as you save the document, you have generated a computer file.

To differentiate one file from another, you must save each file under a unique name—a file name. A file name is any combination of up to eight valid characters (MYFILE, for example). Valid characters include letters of the alphabet (upper- or lowercase), digits 0 through 9, the underscore, and some special characters. If you provide a name longer than eight characters, some application programs give you an error message, others truncate the name and accept only the first eight characters. In addition to a file name, a file is usually saved with a file extension (MYFILE.TXT, for example). Some application programs automatically provide a file extension when you save the file. In other application programs, providing a file extension is the user's responsibility.

There are several characters that have special meanings in different application software. The asterisk (*) can represent up to eight characters. The question mark (?) can represent any single character. These two characters are called **wild card** characters. These wild cards can significantly improve your efficiency while working with application programs. For example, all your 1-2-3 graphics files are identified by *.PIC. The * represents any file name, and the PIC indicates that your file is a 1-2-3 graphics file.

As an illustration of the usefulness of these wild card characters, suppose that you want to copy all your 1-2-3 graphics files from the disk in drive A to the disk in drive B. You would simply type the DOS command COPY *.PIC B:. If the * wild card feature was not available, you would have to type the COPY command as many times as the number of graphics files.

1–14 TYPES OF DATA

Any application program or computer language accepts different types of data. The most commonly used data types are numeric and alphanumeric.

Numeric data include any combination of digits 0 through 9 and decimal points. Numeric data can be integer or real. Integer data include only whole numbers without any decimal points, for example, 656 or 986. Real data include digits and decimal points, 696.25 or 729.793, for example. Real data are sometimes called floating point data, which means the decimal point can move—222.2, 22.22, or 2.222, for example. Another type of real data is fixed point data, which means that the decimal point is always fixed.

Nonnumeric, or alphanumeric, **data** (sometimes called labels or strings) include any types of valid characters. For example, Jackson or 123 Broadway Street. Remember, you cannot perform any arithmetic operations with nonnumeric data or labels.

1–15 TYPES OF VALUES

Computers usually handle two types of values: variables and constants.

Variables are valid computer addresses (locations) that hold different values at different times. For example, when you specify A=65, A is the variable and 65 is the constant. When you specify B="Brown", B is the variable and Brown is the constant. As soon as you enter a new value into this variable, the old value disappears. The **constant** is always fixed. Figure 1–10 illustrates this concept.

Figure 1–10
An Example of a Variable and a Constant

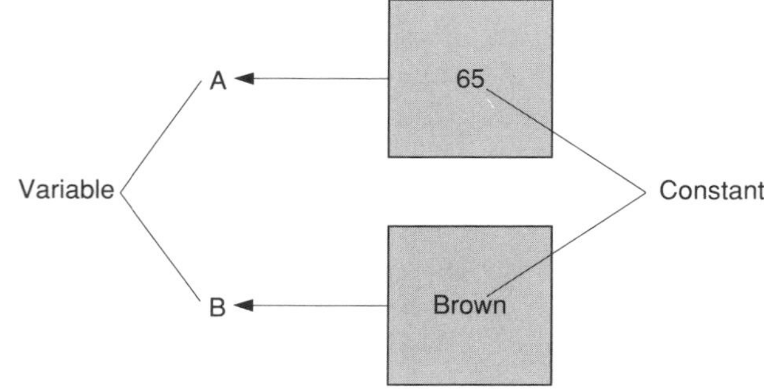

1–16

TYPES OF FORMULAS

There are two types of formulas or functions handled by computers: user-defined and built-in.

User-defined formulas or functions are a combination of computer addresses designed to perform a certain task. For example, the area of a triangle can be presented as A=B*H/2 meaning base multiplied by height divided by 2. In this case, A is a formula or a function. You can enter different values for B and H and a different value for A (the area of the triangle) will be calculated.

Built-in formulas or functions are already available within the application program or the computer language. As soon as the user provides values for a given variable or variables, the application program or the computer language calculates these formulas. For example, SQRT(X) is a function that calculates the square root of a variable, X. The X or any other information needed by these functions is called an argument. As soon as you provide a value for X, the square root is immediately calculated. For example, SQRT(25) is equal to 5. The function FV(payment,interest rate,term) calculates the future value of a series of equal payments with a given interest rate over a period of time (term).

1–17

PRIORITY (PRECEDENCE) OF OPERATIONS

When application programs perform arithmetic operations, they follow a series of rules. These **priority rules** are as follows:

1. Expressions inside parentheses have the highest priority.
2. Exponentiation (raising to power) is performed next.
3. Multiplication and division have the third highest priority.
4. Addition and subtraction have the lowest priority.
5. When there are two or more operations with the same priority, operations proceed from left to right.

The following examples should make this clear. A program uses * for multiplication, ^ for exponentiation, and / for division. If A=5, B=10, and C=2, a computer will calculate the following answers:

```
A+B/C=10
(A+B)/C=7.5
A*B/C=25
(A*B)/C=25
A^C/2=12.50
```

SUMMARY

In this chapter we discussed microcomputers in general. Input and output, and primary and secondary memory devices were explained. General capabilities of microcomputers were introduced, and we presented a series of guidelines for successful selection and maintenance of a microcomputer. We discussed the advantages of microcomputers compared to mainframe computers. The chapter concluded with a hands-on session. We explained computer files, data, values, formulas, and the priority of operations.

REVIEW QUESTIONS

*These questions are answered in Appendix A.

1. What is a microcomputer? What components does a typical minicomputer have?
*2. What are some typical input devices for a PC ?
3. What are some typical output devices for a PC?
4. What is the difference between a primary memory device and a secondary memory device?
5. What is RAM? ROM? PROM? EPROM?
*6. What is the most commonly used secondary memory device for a PC?
7. What are optical technologies? What are their advantages?
8. How do you measure the memory capacity of a PC?
9. Besides memory, what other attributes are important when you buy a computer?
10. What is the difference between a floppy and a hard disk?
11. What is the speed range for a typical microcomputer?
*12. What is the memory size of a typical personal computer?
13. What constitutes good software?
14. What constitutes good hardware?
15. What factors constitute a good contract?
*16. List important things to do when caring for your computer.
17. What are some application programs for a PC?
18. What are some of the advantages of a personal computer compared to a mainframe computer?
19. What is permanent memory in a PC? What is temporary memory?
20. How do you send information from RAM to a disk?
*21. How do you correct your mistakes?
22. What is a computer file?
23. What is a wild card character?
24. Name some different types of data.
25. What is a variable? A constant?
*26. What is priority of operations?
27. What symbols are used for arithmetic operations?
28. Turn on a PC. What do you see? Turn it off. Insert the DOS disk in drive A and turn the computer back on. What do you see this time?
29. Enter the correct date and time into your computer. What happens if you make a mistake?
30. Type DIR and press Enter. What is displayed?
31. How many generations of micros have we seen? What are the most powerful PCs on the market?
32. What types of PCs do you have on your campus? Describe different input/output devices used by the PCs in your school micro lab. Do you have a Bernoulli Box in the lab? What are some of the advantages of a Bernoulli Box over a hard disk?

33. What are the most commonly used disks on your campus? 3-½ or 5-¼? Compare and contrast these two types of storage devices.
34. Consult computer magazines to find out which computer at the present time is using optical disks.
35. Out of 10 application software packages introduced in this chapter, which ones are available on your campus? What are the applications of each?
36. If you want to buy a PC for your personal use, how do you start shopping? What attributes make a PC attractive?

KEY TERMS

Accounting software
Built-in formulas
CD ROM
Communications software
Computer-aided design
Constants
Database software
EPROM
Erasable optical disk
File
Financial planning software
Floppy disk
Graphics software
Hard disk
Input device
Microcomputer
Nonnumeric data
Numeric data
Output device
Permanent area
Primary memory
Priority rules
Project-management software
PROM
RAM
ROM
Secondary memory
Spreadsheet software
User-defined formulas
Variables
Wild card
Word processor
WORM

ARE YOU READY TO MOVE ON?

Multiple Choice

1. Choose the correct ranking of monitor display resolutions from lowest to highest:
   - **a.** VGA, CGA, EGA
   - **b.** EGA, VGA, CGA
   - **c.** EGA, CGA, VGA
   - **d.** CGA, EGA, VGA
   - **e.** none of the above
2. Which of the following is not a typical adapter card?
   - **a.** printer interface card
   - **b.** clock card
   - **c.** disk drive card
   - **d.** display card
   - **e.** punch card
3. Of the various types of main memory, the user has direct control over
   - **a.** ROM
   - **b.** REM
   - **c.** RAM
   - **d.** PROM
   - **e.** all of the above

4. At the present time, the most commonly used secondary storage device is the
   - **a.** 5-¼ inch floppy disk
   - **b.** 3-½ inch floppy disk
   - **c.** Bernoulli Box
   - **d.** hard disk
   - **e.** none of the above
5. The major advantage(s) of optical storage technology is (are)
   - **a.** storage capacity
   - **b.** cost
   - **c.** durability
   - **d.** both a and c
   - **e.** all of the above
6. When we refer to memory and storage capacity sizes, we use the term K (as in 360K). 1K equals approximately
   - **a.** 1 byte
   - **b.** 1,000 bytes
   - **c.** 1,000,000 bytes
   - **d.** 1,048,576 bytes
   - **e.** none of the above
7. Word size directly affects
   - **a.** the speed of the computer
   - **b.** the ability of the user to understand what is being said
   - **c.** the maximum amount of data that can be displayed on the CRT
   - **d.** the choice of which type of disk drive to use
   - **e.** the meaning of the function keys on the keyboard
8. Which of the following are disadvantages of mainframes when compared to microcomputers?
   - **a.** they are more difficult to use
   - **b.** they are more threatening to non-computer users
   - **c.** the user has less control
   - **d.** they are relatively more expensive
   - **e.** all of the above
9. After "booting" the computer with the DOS disk (loading DOS and entering the date and time), you are at
   - **a.** the Lotus Access Menu
   - **b.** the DOS prompt (A>)
   - **c.** the parallel/serial interface
   - **d.** the BASIC prompt
   - **e.** none of the above
10. An example of alphanumeric data would be
    - **a.** 123
    - **b.** 123.
    - **c.** LOTUS-123
    - **d.** A=(123−2)/4
    - **e.** none of the above

True/False

1. The terms personal computer, PC, and microcomputer refer to different types of computers.
2. A typical microcomputer consists of input, output, and memory devices.
3. Monochrome (or amber) CRTs cannot generate graphic output.
4. The purpose of function keys and special keys on a computer keyboard do not vary in different application programs.
5. The capacity of a hard disk is greater than the capacity of a floppy disk.
6. A WORM drive can be recorded and erased repeatedly when high volume storage and updating are essential.
7. Typical microcomputer software packages and applications include spreadsheet, database, graphics, communications, and word processing.
8. The first step in selecting a microcomputer is to define your needs, then think about software.
9. The commands DIR *.* and DIR ????????.??? produce the same results.
10. Expressions inside parentheses have the lowest priority when it comes to performing arithmetic operations.

ANSWERS

Multiple Choice

1. d
2. e
3. c
4. b
5. d
6. b
7. a
8. e
9. b
10. c

True/False

1. F
2. T
3. F
4. F
5. T
6. F
7. T
8. T
9. T
10. F

A Quick Trip with MS- and PC-DOS

2–1 INTRODUCTION

In this chapter, we explain the basics of the disk operating system (DOS). We define the differences between internal and external DOS commands, and explain how you use system time and date. We review file specifications in the DOS environment and discuss how to use the DIR command. Important keys are highlighted, and you learn how to create a data disk using the FORMAT command. We also review the different versions of MS- and PC-DOS. The chapter concludes with a table summarizing most of the important DOS commands.[1]

2–2 TURNING ON YOUR PC

When you access a personal computer, it is either on or off. If the computer is off, put the DOS disk into drive A and turn on the computer (DOS comes with the computer). This procedure is called a **cold boot** (boot means starting the computer).

If the computer is already on, insert the DOS disk into drive A and press Ctrl-Alt-Del (press all three keys simultaneously). This procedure is called a **warm boot**. A warm boot is faster than a cold boot because the computer does not check its memory when you do a warm boot.

When the computer is booted, it prompts you for the current date. Enter the date in the format requested (mm-dd-yy) and press Enter. Next, the computer requests the current time. Enter the time in the correct format (hh:mm:ss) and press Enter. Remember that DOS operates on a 24-hour clock. This means that 2:30 p.m., for example, is entered as 14:30.

You should see the A> prompt, which indicates that the necessary portions of DOS have been loaded into random-access memory (RAM) and drive A is the default drive. Default means that this is the drive the computer will use unless you indicate otherwise. If DOS is installed on your hard disk (which is usually drive C), your default drive will be C.

You can avoid entering the date and time by pressing Enter at the prompts. Your PC will then use the default date and time when saving files. However, it is a good habit to enter the correct date and time each time you start your computer. That way you know your files will be saved with the current time and date stamps. The correct date and time help you determine the most or least recent versions of your files in a directory. (A directory is a listing of all your files.)

If you forget to enter the current date and time at boot-up, you can enter this information at any time with the DATE and TIME commands. At the A> prompt, type *DATE* and press Enter. The computer prompts you to enter the current date in the format mm-dd-yy. Type the date and press Enter. To enter the current time, type *TIME* at the A> prompt and press Enter. You are prompted to enter a new time in the format hh:mm:ss. Then press Enter. The computer holds this information in memory and updates it automatically until you turn off your computer. Some computers have a battery-operated clock on

[1]For a detailed discussion of DOS commands, see *Information Systems Literacy and Software Productivity Tools: DOS* by Hossein Bidgoli (Macmillan, 1991).

their motherboard, which keeps the time and date current even when the computer is turned off.

Internal commands (sometimes called memory-resident commands) are those commands that are loaded into the computer at boot-up. You can use internal commands without the DOS disk in a drive. CLS (clear screen) is an example of an internal DOS command. If you type *CLS* and press Enter, your screen is cleared.

External commands (sometimes called non-memory-resident commands) are those commands that you can execute only when the DOS disk is in a drive. These commands are sometimes called DOS utilities. They are separate programs stored on the DOS disk. DISKCOPY (disk copy), for example, is an external DOS command. You can find a listing of most of these commands at the end of this chapter.

2–3 DOS PROMPTS

Depending on how you start your computer, you will see different prompts. If you have a hard disk and you boot your system from it, your prompt will probably be C>. The prompt indicates the current default drive. The computer uses the default drive unless you specify a different one. Changing the default drive is an easy task. For example, if the default drive is A (indicated by the A> prompt) and you want to change it to drive B, at the A> prompt, type *B:* and press Enter. You prompt should now be B>. To change it back, type *A:* and press Enter. You can customize the DOS prompt with the PROMPT command.

2–4 DOS FILE SPECIFICATIONS

DOS files follow the same general naming conventions as other software. A DOS file name can be up to eight characters long and can contain the digits 0 through 9, as well as special characters, such as an underscore (_) and a pound sign (#). Usually, you should avoid using special symbols.

File extensions can be up to three characters long, and they follow the same conventions as file names. Important file extensions in the DOS environment include the following:

- BAK—Backup files are generated by some word processing, spreadsheet, and database management programs. BAK files are backup copies of original files.
- BAT—Batch files are text files that the user generates. Batch files contain DOS commands that are executed when you type the name of the file.
- COM—Command files can be executed by typing the name of the file.
- EXE—Like COM files, you run executable files by typing the file name.
- SYS—System files can be used only by DOS.

2–5 THE DIR COMMAND

If you type *DIR* and press Enter, you will receive a listing of your current directory. It will resemble the listing shown in figure 2–1. At the top of this

Figure 2–1
A Directory Listing

```
DIR

 Volume in drive A is MSDOS_330A
 Directory of  A:\

ANSI     SYS      1647   3-01-88    8:00a
APPEND   EXE      5794   3-01-88    8:00a
ASSIGN   COM      1530   3-01-88    8:00a
ATTRIB   EXE     10656   3-01-88    8:00a
CHKDSK   COM      9819   3-01-88    8:00a
COMMAND  COM     25308   3-01-88    8:00a
COMP     COM      4183   3-01-88    8:00a
COUNTRY  SYS     11254   3-01-88    8:00a
DISKCOMP COM      5848   3-01-88    8:00a
DISKCOPY COM      6264   3-01-88    8:00a
DISPLAY  SYS     11259   3-01-88    8:00a
DRIVER   SYS      1165   3-01-88    8:00a
EDLIN    COM      7495   3-01-88    8:00a
EXE2BIN  EXE      3050   3-01-88    8:00a
FASTOPEN EXE      3888   3-01-88    8:00a
FDISK    COM     48983   3-01-88    8:00a
FIND     EXE      6403   3-01-88    8:00a
FORMAT   COM     11671   3-01-88    8:00a
GRAFTABL COM      6136   3-01-88    8:00a
GRAPHICS COM     13943   3-01-88    8:00a
JOIN     EXE      9612   3-01-88    8:00a
KEYB     COM      9041   3-01-88    8:00a
LABEL    COM      2346   3-01-88    8:00a
MODE     COM     15440   3-01-88    8:00a
MORE     COM       282   3-01-88    8:00a
NLSFUNC  EXE      3029   3-01-88    8:00a
PRINT    COM      9011   3-01-88    8:00a
RECOVER  COM      4268   3-01-88    8:00a
SELECT   COM      4132   3-01-88    8:00a
SORT     EXE      1946   3-01-88    8:00a
SUBST    EXE     10552   3-01-88    8:00a
SYS      COM      4725   3-01-88    8:00a
TREE     COM      3540   3-01-88    8:00a
       33 File(s)     19456 bytes free

A>
```

figure, you can see that the volume in drive A is MSDOS-3.30A, which is the internal name for this disk. You can use the LABEL command to change the volume names of your disks.

The DIR command displays the name of each file, the file extension, the size of the file in bytes, and the date and time at which the file was created. At the end of the listing, you see the number of files in the current directory and the number of bytes available on the disk.

You can use the DIR command with wild card characters. DOS accepts the asterisk (*) and the question mark (?) as wild cards. These characters substitute for other characters in the file name or extension. The ? substitutes for only one character; the * can substitute for one or more characters. For example, if you type

DIR PLAN?.MON

DOS lists all the files that begin with PLAN and end with .MON, such as PLAN1.MON, PLAN2.MON, or PLANA.MON. If you type

DIR *.MON

DOS lists all the .MON files, such as LETTER.MON, 123.MON, or CHART_1.MON.

2–6 USING DIR WITH SWITCHES

You can use the DIR command with different switches (parameters) to provide different types of listings. The /W switch lists your files in a wide format. Only the file names and extensions are listed. For example, we generated the wide listing of our drive A shown in figure 2–2 by placing our DOS disk in drive A and typing *DIR/W*.

When you use the /P switch, DOS pauses when a directory listing fills your screen and waits for you to press a key before it continues listing files. In figure 2–3, we used the DIR/P command to display the directory of drive A.

You can use the DIR command to list files on any drive, regardless of whether it is the current drive. For example, if your current drive is A and you want to see a listing of drive B, type

DIR B:

Remember to include at least one space between the DIR command and the drive name.

2–7 IMPORTANT KEYS IN THE DOS ENVIRONMENT

Figure 2–4 shows a typical PC keyboard. Several keys perform special tasks in the DOS environment. Table 2–1 lists these keys and their functions.

```
DIR/W

 Volume in drive A is MSDOS_330A
 Directory of  A:\

ANSI     SYS    APPEND   EXE    ASSIGN   COM    ATTRIB   EXE    CHKDSK   COM
COMMAND  COM    COMP     COM    COUNTRY  SYS    DISKCOMP COM    DISKCOPY COM
DISPLAY  SYS    DRIVER   SYS    EDLIN    COM    EXE2BIN  EXE    FASTOPEN EXE
FDISK    COM    FIND     EXE    FORMAT   COM    GRAFTABL COM    GRAPHICS COM
JOIN     EXE    KEYB     COM    LABEL    COM    MODE     COM    MORE     COM
NLSFUNC  EXE    PRINT    COM    RECOVER  COM    SELECT   COM    SORT     EXE
SUBST    EXE    SYS      COM    TREE     COM
       33 File(s)     19456 bytes free

A>
```

Figure 2–2
A Wide Directory Listing

Figure 2–3
Pausing a Directory Listing

```
DIR/P

 Volume in drive A is MSDOS_330A
 Directory of  A:\

ANSI     SYS     1647   3-01-88   8:00a
APPEND   EXE     5794   3-01-88   8:00a
ASSIGN   COM     1530   3-01-88   8:00a
ATTRIB   EXE    10656   3-01-88   8:00a
CHKDSK   COM     9819   3-01-88   8:00a
COMMAND  COM    25308   3-01-88   8:00a
COMP     COM     4183   3-01-88   8:00a
COUNTRY  SYS    11254   3-01-88   8:00a
DISKCOMP COM     5848   3-01-88   8:00a
DISKCOPY COM     6264   3-01-88   8:00a
DISPLAY  SYS    11259   3-01-88   8:00a
DRIVER   SYS     1165   3-01-88   8:00a
EDLIN    COM     7495   3-01-88   8:00a
EXE2BIN  EXE     3050   3-01-88   8:00a
FASTOPEN EXE     3888   3-01-88   8:00a
FDISK    COM    48983   3-01-88   8:00a
FIND     EXE     6403   3-01-88   8:00a
FORMAT   COM    11671   3-01-88   8:00a
GRAFTABL COM     6136   3-01-88   8:00a
GRAPHICS COM    13943   3-01-88   8:00a
JOIN     EXE     9612   3-01-88   8:00a
KEYB     COM     9041   3-01-88   8:00a
LABEL    COM     2346   3-01-88   8:00a
Strike a key when ready . . .
MODE     COM    15440   3-01-88   8:00a
MORE     COM      282   3-01-88   8:00a
NLSFUNC  EXE     3029   3-01-88   8:00a
PRINT    COM     9011   3-01-88   8:00a
RECOVER  COM     4268   3-01-88   8:00a
SELECT   COM     4132   3-01-88   8:00a
SORT     EXE     1946   3-01-88   8:00a
SUBST    EXE    10552   3-01-88   8:00a
SYS      COM     4725   3-01-88   8:00a
TREE     COM     3540   3-01-88   8:00a
       33 File(s)     19456 bytes free

A>
```

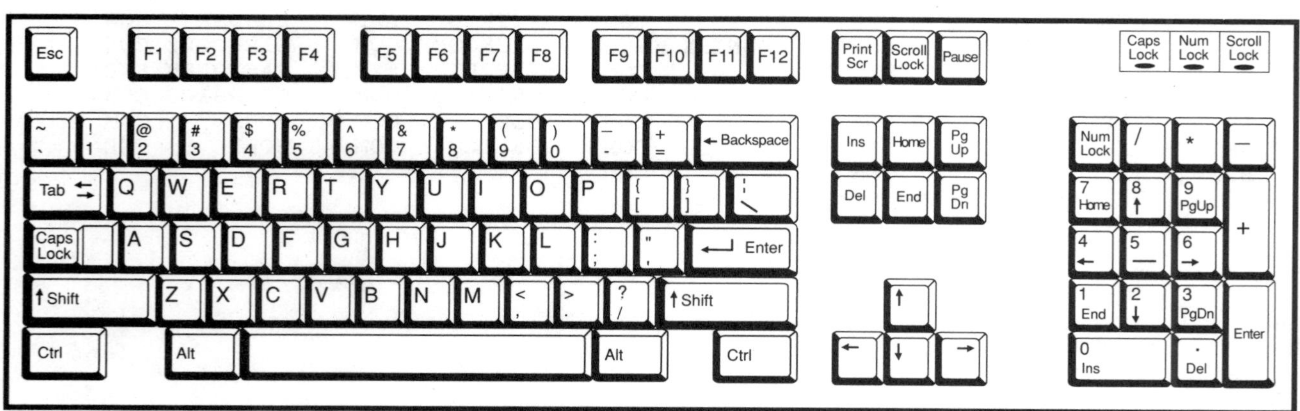

Figure 2–4
A PC Keyboard

Table 2–1
Special Keyboard Keys

Key	Description
Ctrl-Alt-Del	Warm boots your system. Equivalent to turning your computer off, and then on.
Ctrl-C or Ctrl-Break	Cancels a command while it is being executed.
Ctrl-PrtSc or Ctrl-P	Sends a copy of each line on-screen to the printer as it is displayed. This command is a toggle; it remains in effect until you press it again.
Shift-PrtSc (or PrtSc on enhanced keyboards)	Sends a copy of the entire screen to the printer. This command is not a toggle.
Ctrl-S or Ctrl-Num Lock	Pauses the directory listing for viewing.
F1 function key	Displays one character of the previous command with each press. Useful for editing a DOS command.
F3 function key	Displays the previous command. Useful for repetitive tasks.
Esc	Erases the current command or statement.

2–8 THE FORMAT COMMAND

Before you can use a new disk on your computer, it must be formatted. To format a disk, place the DOS disk into drive A, type

FORMAT A:

and press Enter. Remove the DOS disk, insert the disk to be formatted into drive A, and press Enter. When DOS is finished formatting the disk, you are asked if you want to format another. If you answer yes, you are prompted to insert another disk. If you answer no, the DOS prompt reappears.

When you format a disk, DOS checks it for defective spots and tells you whether the disk is usable. The FORMAT command also divides a disk into tracks and sectors, and creates a File Allocation Table (FAT). The FAT tells DOS where the data are stored on the disk.

When you format a disk, everything on it is erased. Make sure that the disk you are formatting is either brand new or contains files that you no longer need.

Figure 2–5 shows what your screen looks like when you have completed formatting a disk in drive A. You also can format a disk in a different drive. For

```
A>FORMAT A:
Insert new diskette for drive A:
and strike ENTER when ready

Format complete

    362496 bytes total disk space
    362496 bytes available on disk

Format another (Y/N)?N
A>
```

Figure 2–5
Formatting a Disk in Drive A

example, if you have your DOS disk in drive A, you can format a disk in drive B by typing

FORMAT B:

2–9
DIFFERENT VERSIONS OF MS- AND PC-DOS

PC-DOS is used with the IBM computer, and MS-DOS is used with IBM-compatible computers. Both versions have evolved through several levels. Major versions are numbered 1.0, 2.0, 3.0, and so forth. Minor revisions are numbered 1.01, 2.2, 3.02, and so on. The current version is 5.0. Each new version has added new commands and corrected the bugs in previous versions. Versions 3.1 and later include commands for a LAN (Local Area Network).

Versions of MS- and PC-DOS are upwardly compatible, which means that all the commands in earlier versions are available in later versions. To a typical microcomputer user, PC-DOS and MS-DOS are almost identical. To find out which version of DOS you are using, type *VER* and press Enter. Figure 2–6 illustrates this process. As you can see, our version of DOS is 3.3. All commands discussed in this book work with all versions of DOS unless otherwise specified.

2–10
BATCH AND AUTOEXEC FILES

Batch files contain a series of DOS commands that are executed as if you typed them individually. These files are helpful when you must perform repetitive operations. A batch file can have any standard name and the extension must always be BAT. Batch files can be any length, and you can include any valid command or statement. To generate a batch file, you can use EDLIN (the DOS line editor) or any word processing program.

For simple files, you can use a version of the copy command as follows:

COPY CON MYFILE.BAT
command or statement
command or statement
command or statement

You must press Enter after each command or statement in your batch file. To end a batch file, press Ctrl-Z or the F6 function key. To execute a batch file, insert the disk containing the file into your default drive and type the name of the file.

Figure 2–6
Displaying the DOS Version

```
A>VER

MS-DOS Version 3.30

A>
```

Enter the following batch file at the A> prompt, pressing keys as indicated:

COPY CON HELLO.BAT (Enter)
DIR (Enter)
CLS (Enter)
BASICA (Enter)(Ctrl-Z)

If you type *HELLO* at the A> prompt, you will see a directory of that drive, the screen will clear, and BASICA will be loaded into RAM (assuming that the disk in drive A contains BASICA).

The only limitation with using the COPY CON command is that you cannot edit your batch file. You must recreate the entire file or import the file created by COPY CON into EDLIN or a word processing program to make changes.

To stop execution of your batch file, press Ctrl-Break.

You can have your batch file execute automatically when you start your computer system by naming it AUTOEXEC.BAT. DOS always looks for this file first. You can use this file to create custom menus for your system, to load a particular program that you use frequently, or anything else you want to have done automatically when you first turn on your computer.

Table 2–2 lists some DOS commands and their functions. In this table, we assume that you are working from the A> prompt. A means drive A, B means drive B, ext stands for any valid file extension, and filename stands for any valid file name.

Table 2–2
Important DOS Commands

Command	Function
ATTRIB +R filename.ext	Makes a file a read-only file (Release 3 and higher)
ATTRIB -R filename.ext	Removes the read-only status (Release 3 and higher)
CHDIR (CD)	Changes the current directory or displays the current path
CHKDSK	Displays amount of free disk space or the amount of free memory on your computer
CHKDSK B:	Displays amount of free disk space in drive B
CLS	Clears the screen
COMP A:filename.ext B:filename.ext	Compares two files
COPY filename.ext B:	Copies filename.ext to drive B
COPY B:filename.ext	Copies filename.ext to drive A
COPY *.ext B:	Copies all files with the ext extension from A to B
COPY B:*.ext	Copies all files with the ext extension from B to A
COPY *.* B:	Copies all files from A to B

Table 2–2 *(Continued)*

Command	Function
COPY B:*.*	Copies all files from B to A
COPY filename1.ext filename2.ext	Copies a file from A to A with a different name
COPY filename1.ext B:filename2.ext	Copies a file from A to B with a different name
COPY B:filename1.ext filename2.ext	Copies a file from B to A with a different name
COPY CON B:filename.BAT	Creates a batch file in drive B
Ctrl-Alt-Del	Resets system (warm boot)
DATE	Sets system date
DEL filename.ext	Erases filename.ext from A
DEL B:filename.ext	Erases filename.ext from B
DEL B:filename.*	Erases filename with any extension from B
DEL B:*.ext	Erases files with the same extension from B
DIR	Displays directory of A
DIR B:	Displays directory of B
DIR/P	Pauses while displaying directory of A
DIR B:/P	Pauses while displaying directory of B
DIR/W	Displays directory of A in wide format
DIR B:/W	Displays directory of B in wide format
DIR | SORT	Displays a sorted directory of A
DIR B: | SORT	Displays a sorted directory of B
DISKCOPY A: B:	Copies disk in A to disk in B
DISKCOMP	Compares two disks, track by track and sector by sector to determine whether the contents are identical
ERASE filename.ext	Erases filename.ext on A
ERASE B:filename.ext	Erases filename.ext on B
ERASE *.ext	Erases all files with same extension on A
ERASE B:*.ext	Erases all files with same extension on B
FORMAT	Formats disk in A
FORMAT B:	Formats disk in B
FORMAT/V	Formats disk in A with volume label
FORMAT B:/V	Formats disk in B with volume label
LABEL	Creates, changes, or deletes a volume label
MKDIR (MD)	Creates a subdirectory
PATH	Searches a specified directory for a program that cannot be found in current directory
PROMPT	Customizes DOS system prompt
RENAME filename1.ext filename2.ext	Renames a file on A

Table 2–2 *(Continued)*

Command	Function
RENAME B:filename1.ext filename2.ext	Renames a file on B
RMDIR (RD)	Removes a subdirectory
Shift-PrtSc (PrtSc on enhanced keyboards)	Prints the screen
SYS	Places operating system files (IBM.DOS and IBMBIO.COM) on the disk specified
TIME	Sets system time
TREE	Displays structure of current directory
TYPE filename.ext	Displays contents of filename.ext
TYPE B:filename.ext	Displays contents of filename.ext on B
VER	Displays DOS version
VERIFY	Checks data just written to disk to be sure the data has been recorded correctly
VERIFY ON/VERIFY OFF	Sets verify status
VOL	Displays volume label of disk (if label exists)

SUMMARY

This chapter reviewed simple DOS operations. We explained the difference between internal and external DOS commands, and we discussed the types of DOS prompts and file name specifications. You learned how to use the DIR command with various switches and how to format a disk using FORMAT.

WordPerfect at a Glance

3

3–1 INTRODUCTION

In this chapter we introduce WordPerfect—one of the most popular word processing programs on the market. The different generations of word ssing machines are introduced, and we explain the capabilities of WordPerfect. We highlight the help facilities included with WordPerfect. After outlining the general aspects of WordPerfect, we introduce a complete cycle of word processing operations, including file creation, modification, saving, printing, retrieving, and exiting the program. We also present an overview of the WordPerfect pull-down menu.

In the next chapter, we introduce more advanced operations with WordPerfect. In this book we cover WordPerfect 5.1. At the end of each chapter in this section, the specific differences between Wordperfect 4.2, 5.0, and 5.1 are highlighted. We give a complete listing of all the commands for Wordperfect 4.2 and 5.0 in addition to a command map for WordPerfect 5.1 in the WordPerfect appendix.

3–2 WORD PROCESSOR AND TYPEWRITER: A COMPARISON

A **word processor** offers many features not found in a typewriter. A word processor is similar to a typewriter that has a large memory. With a word processor you can create a document, edit it, revise it, do cutting and pasting, save it on disk, and, finally, print it on a printer. Using a word processor you do not need to use liquid paper to erase an unwanted word, and you do not need scissors to do cutting and pasting! Everything is done electronically with a high degree of efficiency and effectiveness. Throughout this section, you will learn many powerful features of WordPerfect, which is one of the most popular word processing programs on the market.

3–3 A WORD PROCESSING REVOLUTION

Word processors have gone through a major revolution. The earliest word processors were **dedicated word processors—**they were capable of performing only word processing tasks. These machines were relatively expensive. Only medium and large organizations could afford them.

In the past decade, mainframe computers have also performed word processing tasks. A **mainframe-based word processing** system is usually difficult to use and lacks flexibility.

The microcomputer era has brought a new meaning to word processing operations. **Microcomputer-based word processors** are relatively inexpensive and easy to use. These word processors may impose a few limitations when compared to mainframe-based word processors, however. These limitations may include the size and format of a document. For most purposes, microcomputer-based word processors perform major word processing tasks in an efficient and effective manner.

3–4 WORDPERFECT: THE ENTIRE PACKAGE

WordPerfect is considered by many experts to be one of the best word processing programs. The tasks performed by WordPerfect can be classified into five major components: word processor, speller, thesaurus, merge, and advanced features.

The word processor component is a full-featured word processing program. A document can be created, indented, formatted, saved, and printed. Electronic cut and paste, and variable spacing are easily done using this component of the WordPerfect program.

The **speller** component contains a dictionary with over 115,000 words to check your spelling against. Using the speller, you should be able to create documents with no spelling errors.

The **thesaurus** component includes over 15,000 antonyms and synonyms. The thesaurus gives you a series of options from which you can choose.

The **merge** component enables you to merge or combine a "boiler-plate" document with another document. For example, using the merge feature, you can generate a letter with the same content and address it to hundreds or thousands of people. In this case, the first document (the letter) is constant, and the second document (the names and addresses) is variable. The merge feature combines the letter with all these names and addresses to generate a letter for each individual address.

We call the last feature of WordPerfect the advanced features component. Using the advanced features, you can perform math functions, search and sort, draw lines, incorporate graphics into your documents, and develop keyboard macros.

3–5 WORDPERFECT TECHNICAL REQUIREMENTS

WordPerfect is available for PC or PC-compatible machines, such as the IBM PC, NEC Advanced, AT&T, PS/2, Apple Macintosh, and Zenith. A microcomputer with a floppy and a hard disk is required. The minimum memory requirement is 512K, but more memory is recommended.

3–6 STARTING WORDPERFECT

Change the current directory to the subdirectory in which WordPerfect is installed (using the CD\ command), type *WP,* and press Enter. You are presented with the screen shown in figure 3–1.

This screen is called the **data-entry window**. There are 24 lines available for you to type text. You should see the flashing cursor at the upper left corner of the screen. The line at the bottom of the screen (the 25th line) is called the **status line**. It tells you that you are in document 1, page 1, line 1, position 1″. This means that the line that the cursor is on is one inch from the top of the page

```
                                         Doc 1 Pg 1 Ln 1" Pos 1"
```

Figure 3–1
The WordPerfect Data-Entry Window

and one inch from the left edge of the page. When you move the cursor by entering text, the status line changes automatically to reflect the current position of the cursor.

The Pos indicator in the status line tells you other valuable information. If it is displayed as POS, the Caps Lock key is on. If the Pos indicator is blinking, the Num Lock key is in effect. If the number following the Pos indicator appears in bold, the bold feature is on, and if it appears as underlined, this means the underline feature is on.

3–7 YOUR FIRST ELECTRONIC DOCUMENT

To get started with WordPerfect, you must have a formatted disk. In this text, we use a computer equipped with one floppy disk drive and a hard disk. The WordPerfect program is installed in a subdirectory called WP51. Change the directory to this subdirectory by using the CD\WP51 command. Boot WordPerfect from the hard disk by typing *WP* and pressing Enter. Insert a formatted disk into drive A so that you can save your document on it. If you don't specify a drive when you save, Wordperfect will save documents to the default directory (C:\WP51). Type the following two lines:

> Using WordPerfect, we can generate documents that can be revised later. Cut and paste becomes an easy task.

Figure 3–2 illustrates this document. Remember, do not press Enter until after you have typed the word task. WordPerfect will word wrap. This means that as you type and the cursor approaches the right side of the screen, if WordPerfect cannot fit the entire word on one line it moves the entire word to

```
Using WordPerfect we can generate documents that can be revised
later. Cut and paste become an easy task.




A:\WORDPB\CH3-2.WP                          Doc 1 Pg 1 Ln 1.17" Pos 1.5"
```

Figure 3–2
Your First Electronic Document

the next line automatically. At the end of each line WordPerfect places a soft return. The **soft return** marks the end of the line. However, if you want to cut a line short or you want to break a line, you must press Enter. This is called a hard return. A **hard return** marks the end of a line or a paragraph. Each hard return in an empty line inserts a blank line in the text.

In this example, we started from the first available column, at position 1″. If you want to start a paragraph (indent a line), press the Tab key once to move the cursor over five columns (positions) to the 1.5″ position.

At any time you can see 24 lines of your document. When you type a line beyond 24, the first line of the document scrolls off the top of the screen.

3–8 THE ON-LINE HELP FACILITY

WordPerfect provides an impressive **on-line help facility** that can be accessed at any time while you are working with the program by pressing the F3 function key. WordPerfect 5.1 provides context-sensitive help, which means that if you don't remember how to gain access to a particular feature, you can press the F3 to get help with that specific feature.

Figure 3–3 illustrates the start-up screen of the on-line help facility. The help facility is very flexible and powerful. You can ask for specific help on any command or aspect of WordPerfect. If you type E at the start-up screen of the help facility, you see an alphabetical list of all of the E commands, such as Edit and Exit. For help with a specific command, you must type the key(s) corresponding to the command. For example, type *E* to display all the E commands in the middle column. Next, you can press the key corresponding to

```
Help                                                WP 5.1   11/06/89

     Press any letter to get an alphabetical list of features.

          The list will include the features that start with that letter,
          along with the name of the key where the feature is found.  You
          can then press that key to get a description of how the feature
          works.

     Press any function key to get information about the use of the key.

          Some keys may let you choose from a menu to get more information
          about various options.  Press HELP again to display the template.

Selection: 0                                      (Press ENTER to exit Help)
```

Figure 3–3
The Start-Up Menu of the On-Line Help Facility

```
Exit

     Gives you the option to save your document and then allows you to either
     exit WordPerfect or clear the screen.

     Exit is also used to exit from editing headers, styles, footnotes, etc.

     When you are in screens other than editing screens, pressing Exit leaves
     menus and will normally take you back to the normal editing screen (you
     may need to press Exit more than once).

Selection: 0                                          (Press ENTER to exit Help)
```

Figure 3–4
On-Line Help on the Exit Command

the command you need help with. You also can press a function key and WordPerfect will provide you with information on this key. To exit the on-line help facility, press Enter or the spacebar. Figure 3–4 illustrates this specific help facility.

Another help-related feature of WordPerfect is the **keyboard template**. Press F3 twice to get a copy of the template, which you can print out. The template lists 40 of WordPerfect's most commonly used commands, grouped by color. Print the template using the Print Screen (PrtSc) key, cut it out, and put the template over your keyboard. The template is for the old standard keyboards, but the functions and commands are the same for newer, enhanced keyboards. Each command corresponds to a function key. Figure 3–5 illustrates the WordPerfect keyboard command template. This template is included in the WordPerfect package when you purchase it.

3–9 MOVING AROUND THE DOCUMENT

While you are in WordPerfect, you are able to move to any location of your document. Table 3–1 provides a summary of the important cursor control keys.

Remember, when you move from one line to another or from one screen to another, WordPerfect keeps track of the relative position. For example, if you are in position 30 and move to the next screen, the cursor will move to position 30 in the next screen. If the line in the receiving screen is shorter, the cursor moves to the last character position in the receiving screen.

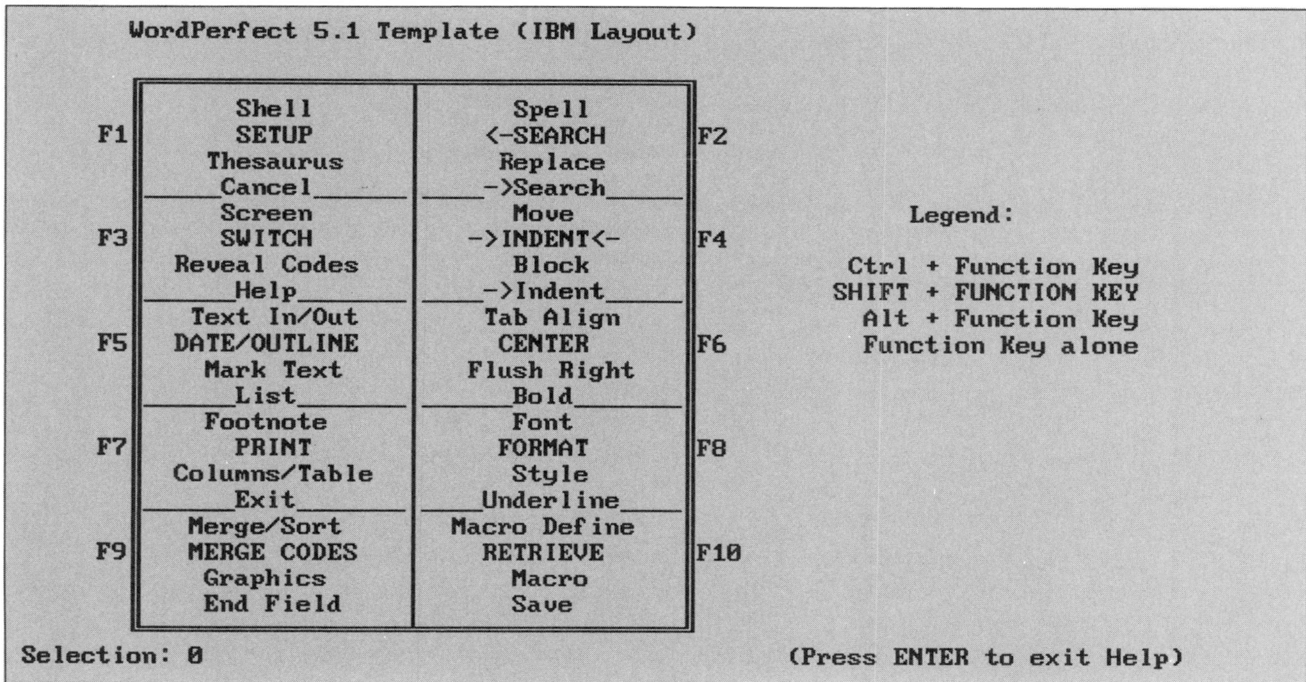

Figure 3–5
WordPerfect Keyboard Command Template

3–10 CORRECTING MISTAKES

If you make a mistake, don't panic. Correcting mistakes using WordPerfect is a very easy task. If you make a mistake and you discover it immediately, you can use the Backspace key to correct it. Each press of the Backspace key erases one character to the left of the cursor. If you discover your mistakes after the document is completely typed, you can use one of the arrow keys to move to the error location. Characters also can be deleted with the Del key, which erases the character the cursor is on.

To insert a series of characters in a WordPerfect document, you have two options. The **insert** option is WordPerfect's default option. This means you can move to any location and type all the characters that were left out. As you type, the existing text is moved to the right. When you finish typing, use the down arrow key to move the cursor down one line and the text will be reformatted. The second option is the **typeover** option. This means you can type over the existing text. To activate the typeover option press the Ins (insert) key once. You will see that the word Typeover is displayed on the status line. To exit this mode, press the Ins key once again.

To see how these two options work, move the cursor to the beginning of the word "documents" (see fig. 3–2). Suppose that you want to replace "documents" with "reports." Press the Ins key to activate the typeover mode. Now type *reports.* Press Ins again to exit the typeover mode. You can eliminate the two additional characters (ts) with the Del key. Press Del twice. The extra characters disappear and their spaces are closed up. Now type *or any other word processing program* after "WordPerfect." Move the cursor to the position just after

Table 3–1
Cursor Control Keys

Key	Function
→	Moves the cursor one position to right
←	Moves the cursor one position to left
↑	Moves the cursor one line up
↓	Moves the cursor one line down
Ctrl-→	Moves the cursor to the first character of the next word to the right
Ctrl-←	Moves the cursor to the first character of the next word to the left
End	Moves the cursor to the end of the line
Home-→	Moves the cursor to the end of the line where the cursor is residing
Home-←	Moves the cursor to the beginning of the line where the cursor is residing
Home-Home-→	Moves the cursor to the extreme right border of the document
Home-Home-←	Moves the cursor to the extreme left border of the document
− (minus)	Moves the cursor up one screen (24 lines) (Num Lock must be off)
+ (plus)	Moves the cursor down one screen (24 lines) (Num Lock must be off)
Ctrl-Home #	Moves the cursor to the top of a given page (page is defined by #)
Home-Home-↑	Moves the cursor to the beginning of the document
Home-Home-Home-↑	Moves the cursor to the extreme beginning of the document
Home-Home-↓	Moves the cursor to the end of the document
PgDn	Moves the cursor to the first line on the next page of the document
PgUp	Moves the cursor to the first line on the previous page of the document

the character "t" in "WordPerfect." Type *or any other word processing program*. You will see that when you type, the existing text is moved to the right. When you are finished typing, move the cursor down one line and the text will be reformatted. The final output is shown in figure 3–6. To slide the existing text to the right by one position, you should press the spacebar key once.

To correct your mistakes, you should know other versions of the Delete command. Table 3–2 provides a summary of these commands.

When Ctrl-End is used to erase a line and the line contains a soft carriage return, the text below is moved up and the blank line disappears. However, a line that contains a hard return at the end stays empty after it is erased. To eliminate the line completely you must erase the hard return by using the Del key.

While you are using this Delete command, remember that WordPerfect saves the last three deletions you performed. To restore deleted text, move the cursor to the position where you would like to reinsert the deleted text, and then press the F1 function key. You see the following menu:

```
Undelete: 1     Restore; 2     Previous Deletion: 0
```

```
Using WordPerfect or any other word processing program, we can
generate reports that can be revised later. Cut and paste become an
easy task.





A:\WORDPB\CH3-6.WP                         Doc 1 Pg 1 Ln 1.17" Pos 7.4"
```

Figure 3–6
Revised Version of the Example Electronic Document

The most recently deleted text will be displayed at the cursor location. If this is the correct text, press 1; otherwise press 2. The 0 option cancels the restoration operation.

3–11 SAVING YOUR DOCUMENT ON DISK

To save your file on disk, press the F10 function key. After issuing the F10 command, you must provide a drive or directory identifier and a file name. This procedure saves your document on disk and returns you to the document. You also should use a file extension. It is a good idea to use WP as the file extension. This will distinguish your WordPerfect files from other files. WordPerfect also

Table 3–2
Summary of Delete Commands

Key	Function
Backspace	Erases one character to the left of the cursor by each press
Ctrl-Backspace	Deletes the word at the cursor position
Ctrl-End	Deletes from cursor position to the end of the line
Ctrl-PgDn	Deletes from cursor position to end of the page (will request confirmation)
Del	Erases the character that the cursor is on
Home-Backspace	Deletes a portion of a word from cursor position to the beginning of the word
Home-Del	Deletes a portion of a word from cursor position to the end of the word

provides an automatic backup feature. This feature must be specified during the installation. The user can define the interval between automatic backups. For example, automatic backups can be performed every 5 minutes, 10 minutes, and so on. It's a good idea to use F10 (the Save key) every 10 minutes or so to protect yourself against unexpected events such as a power failure.

When you press F10, WordPerfect displays the name of the file (if it is already saved). You can press Enter to save the file under its present name. If you do this, WordPerfect displays Replace No(Yes). If you choose Y, it means the new file replaces the old one regardless of any differences in size. If you do not choose the replace option, you must enter a new name for the file to be saved under. Using the F7 function key (Exit) is another method for saving a file. This key saves the document but does not return you to the document. It allows you to stay within WordPerfect and work with a clear screen, or exit WordPerfect to DOS or your starting menu.

3–12 PRINTING A FILE

To print a file, you have two options. The first option is to press Shift-PrtSc. Some enhanced keyboards have a PrtSc key that will print your document without pressing the shift key. This will print one screen at a time. The second option is to use the print command. To do so first make sure that your printer is on and connected, then press the Shift and F7 keys together. When you press Shift and F7, the menu shown in figure 3–7 is displayed.

If you type 1, the full document will be printed using the WordPerfect default print options. You can choose other options from this menu. The WordPerfect default options are summarized in table 3– 3.

Figure 3–7
The Print Menu

```
Print

     1 - Full Document
     2 - Page
     3 - Document on Disk
     4 - Control Printer
     5 - Multiple Pages
     6 - View Document
     7 - Initialize Printer


Options

     S - Select Printer                   HP LaserJet IIP
     B - Binding Offset                   0"
     N - Number of Copies                 1
     U - Multiple Copies Generated by     WordPerfect
     G - Graphics Quality                 Medium
     T - Text Quality                     High



Selection: 0
```

Left margin	1 inch (9 spaces)
Right margin	1 inch (9 spaces)
Top margin	1 inch (6 lines)
Bottom margin	1 inch (6 lines)
Length of the page	54 lines
Starting character	Column 10 or 1″
Ending character	Column 74 or 7.4″
Spacing	Single

Table 3–3
WordPerfect Default Options

3–13 RETRIEVING AN EXISTING FILE

To retrieve a file that is already saved, press Shift-F10 (the Retrieve-Text key) and type the file name. If you have several files on your disk, press the F5 function key (the List Files key) to generate a directory of all your files on the default drive. From here you can then select the desired file. Remember, if you are interested in a drive other than your default drive, you can specify that drive by typing the drive name and pressing Enter. To do this, first press the F5 key, type an equal sign (=), and then specify your new default drive or directory. For example, you can type = *A:* and press Enter to display a directory listing of drive A. Drive A will remain the current drive until you terminate your WordPerfect session or until you change it again using the same method.

Press F5 to see the screen shown in figure 3–8.

```
01-01-91  09:12a              Directory C:\WP51\*.*
Document size:        0  Free:    512,000 Used:  3,732,842      Files:     97

 .    Current     <Dir>                     |  ..   Parent      <Dir>
 CLASS    .       <Dir>  05-16-90 05:08p    |  WP51DATA.        <Dir>  04-30-90 08:32p
 8514A    .VRS    4,866  11-06-89 12:00p    |  ARROW-22.WPG       116  11-06-89 12:00p
 ATI      .VRS    6,041  11-06-89 12:00p    |  BALLOONS.WPG     2,806  11-06-89 12:00p
 BANNER-3.WPG       648  11-06-89 12:00p    |  BICYCLE .WPG       607  11-06-89 12:00p
 BKGRND-1.WPG    11,391  11-06-89 12:00p    |  BORDER-8.WPG       144  11-06-89 12:00p
 BULB     .WPG    2,030  11-06-89 12:00p    |  BURST-1 .WPG       748  11-06-89 12:00p
 BUTTRFLY.WPG     5,278  11-06-89 12:00p    |  CALENDAR.WPG       300  11-06-89 12:00p
 CERTIF   .WPG      608  11-06-89 12:00p    |  CHARACTR.DOC    42,223  11-06-89 12:00p
 CHARMAP  .TST   42,450  11-06-89 12:00p    |  CHKBOX-1.WPG       582  11-06-89 12:00p
 CLOCK    .WPG    1,811  11-06-89 12:00p    |  CNTRCT-2.WPG     2,678  11-06-89 12:00p
 CONVERT  .EXE  105,141  11-06-89 12:00p    |  CURSOR  .COM     1,452  11-06-89 12:00p
 DEVICE-2.WPG       657  11-06-89 12:00p    |  DIPLOMA .WPG     2,342  11-06-89 12:00p
 EGA512   .FRS    3,584  11-06-89 12:00p    |  EGAITAL .FRS     3,584  11-06-89 12:00p
 EGASMC   .FRS    3,584  11-06-89 12:00p    |  EGAUND  .FRS     3,584  11-06-89 12:00p
 EPLQ850  .PRS    9,471  04-30-90 08:28p    |  FINISH  .WPM       252  01-02-91 03:29a
 FINSIH   .WPM       77  01-02-91 03:16a    |  FIXBIOS .COM        50  11-06-89 12:00p
 FLOPPY-2.WPG       404  11-06-89 12:00p    |  GAVEL   .WPG       887  11-06-89 12:00p
 GENIUS   .VRS   12,367  11-06-89 12:00p    ▼  GLOBE2-M.WPG     7,785  11-06-89 12:00p

1 Retrieve; 2 Delete; 3 Move/Rename; 4 Print; 5 Short/Long Display;
6 Look; 7 Other Directory; 8 Copy; 9 Find; N Name Search: 6
```

Figure 3–8
The Retrieve Menu

Table 3–4
RETRIEVE Options

Option	Function
Retrieve	Moves the selected file into memory (RAM)
Delete	Erases a selected file from your directory
Move/Rename	Renames a selected file on your directory
Print	Sends a copy of a selected file to the printer
Short/Long Display	Alters the way that files are listed under the F5 (List Files) key. Long display allows the use of 30-character file names, and allows document type to be included
Look	Views a selected file without loading it into RAM. This command displays one page of the file at a time. Remember, you cannot perform any editing task while you are using the look command
Other Directory	Accesses any other directory besides the default directory
Copy	Copies a selected file into another file, directory, or disk
Find	Displays all of the files that meet a certain condition that the user specifies. It is helpful for maintaining large, complex directory structures
N Name Search	Finds a particular file name quickly. You must press Enter to leave the Name Search feature. You use the spacebar to return to the document screen. Pressing Enter at the beginning menu enables you to look at the current file, because Look is the default option

At the bottom of the screen several options are listed. To select any of these options, move the cursor to the file you want to access, and then select the option by pressing the option number or the highlighted character of the option. Table 3–4 gives a brief description of each option.

3–14 EXITING WORDPERFECT

To exit WordPerfect and save your document, press F7. The prompt on the status line asks whether you would like to save your document. If you choose Yes, you must type the drive identifier or directory and a file name with an extension. Any name up to eight characters can be used. Use WP as the file extension in order to identify that this is a WordPerfect file.

After saving your document, WordPerfect asks whether you would like to exit the program. If you select No, the screen is cleared and you are ready to type a new document. If you choose Yes, you exit WordPerfect and are returned to the operating system or the menu where you started.

3–15 WORDPERFECT APPROACH TO COMMANDS

As you will see in future chapters, all WordPerfect commands are executed by function keys (F1-F12), used alone or used in combination with the Alt, Ctrl, and Shift keys. The appendix contains a complete listing of all WordPerfect commands.

3–16 WORDPERFECT PULL-DOWN MENU

WordPerfect 5.1 offers a significant enhancement over its predecessors through the incorporation of pull-down menus into the program. The pull-down menu can be activated either directly from the keyboard or by using a mouse. In the next few paragraphs we provide you with the information you need in case you decide to use these optional enhancements of WordPerfect 5.1.

To activate the menu from the keyboard, press Alt-=. When you do this, the WordPerfect main menu is displayed as follows:

```
File Edit Search Layout Mark Tools Font Graphics Help
```

Once you are in the pull-down menu, highlight the option you want, then press Enter to select the option. We present a complete command map for WordPerfect 5.1 in the appendix.

3–17 MOUSE SUPPORT FOR WORDPERFECT

If you have a mouse attached to your computer, the pull-down menu can be accessed by "clicking" the right mouse button. Place your hand over the mouse, gently grasping the sides between your thumb and third (ring) finger. Your index finger and middle finger should be resting lightly on the mouse buttons. As you place your hand on the mouse, you may see a small rectangle appear on the screen. This rectangle is called the mouse cursor, and its movements will correspond to the movements of the mouse across your desk or table. With a quick motion, click the right mouse button. A menu bar will appear across the top of your screen, presenting the following options:

```
File Edit Search Layout Mark Tools Font Graphics Help
```

The File option will be highlighted, indicating that it is the current active menu option. Press the down arrow on your keyboard. The pull-down menu for the File option will "cascade" down your screen. Several options will appear under the File menu. The triangle that is next to some of the options indicates that those options have sub-menus associated with them. When you highlight an option with a triangle next to it, the sub-menu associated with that option will automatically appear on your screen. Press the right-arrow key. The File pull-down menu will disappear from the screen, and the Edit menu will appear. Continue pressing the right-arrow key, taking a moment to familiarize yourself with the various options under each pull-down menu. When you reach the Help option at the right side of the menu bar, pressing the right-arrow key once more will wrap the cursor back around to the File option. Click the right mouse button once again to turn off the pull-down menu system.

Instead of using the arrow keys, another method of moving within the pull-down menus is by using the mouse. To do this, first click the right mouse button to access the pull-down menu bar. Point to the File option with the mouse cursor. To point, simply move the mouse across your desk until the mouse cursor is anywhere on the word File (in the menu bar), then click the left mouse button. The File pull-down menu will appear on your screen. Next, point to the Layout menu bar option, and click the left mouse button again. The File pull-down menu disappears, and the Layout pull-down menu appears. Point the mouse cursor at the Tools option, and click left. The Tools pull-down menu replaces the Layout pull-down menu. Move the mouse cursor down into the Tools menu, point the mouse cursor anywhere in the Date Text option, and click left. In the blink of an eye, the system date will appear on your screen at the exact position of the flashing WordPerfect cursor, and the menu bar will disappear.

Another use of the mouse is cursor movement. Rather than using the arrow keys to reposition the cursor within a document, you can simply point the mouse cursor to the new position you wish to move to, then click left. The flashing cursor will automatically reposition itself to the new location. If you hold down the right mouse button and move the mouse cursor to the top or bottom of your screen, the document will automatically scroll up or down, depending upon your direction of movement. Release the mouse button when you have scrolled to the new desired location in your document.

Blocking areas of text can also be easily performed using the mouse. By holding down the left mouse button and moving the mouse cursor, you can automatically block areas of text to prepare them for operations such as moving, copying, bolding, etc. To try this, type a sentence onto the screen. Position the mouse cursor at the beginning of the sentence, hold down the left mouse button, then move the cursor down and to the right. You will see the words "Block on" flashing in the lower left corner of your screen, and WordPerfect will automatically block the sentence for you. With your hand still holding down the left mouse button, move the mouse cursor back toward the beginning of the sentence. As you can see, the blocking feature will follow the movements of the mouse, and by using this method you can select as much or as little text as you want.

3–18 PULL-DOWN MENU HIGHLIGHTS

1. To save a file, from the file menu select Save, specify a file name, then press Enter.
2. To print a file, from the file menu select Print, then press 1 or 2 for full document or page.
3. To retrieve a file, from the file menu Select Retrieve, specify a file name, then press Enter.
4. To exit WordPerfect, from the file menu select Exit, select Yes or No at the Save Document prompt, then press Y to exit WordPerfect.
5. To move around in your document, from the main menu select Search, then select one of the desired options.
6. To receive on-line help, from the main menu select Help, then select Help, Help Index, or Template.

SUMMARY

This chapter provided a quick summary of WordPerfect. Different capabilities of WordPerfect including the help facilities were explained. The entire word processing cycle, including file creation, correction, saving, printing, retrieving, and exiting were explained. The chapter briefly introduced the WordPerfect pull-down menu and the mouse support for this menu. In the next chapter more advanced features of WordPerfect will be introduced.

REVIEW QUESTIONS

*These questions are answered in Appendix A.

1. What are three major advantages of a word processor compared to a typewriter?
2. How were word processing tasks performed 15 years ago?

*3. What are five major capabilities of WordPerfect?

4. What does the thesaurus feature do?

5. What system can run WordPerfect?
6. How do you get the help facility started?
7. How do you start WordPerfect from a hard disk system?
*8. How do you receive on-line help for a specific command?
9. How do you indent a line?
10. How many lines can be displayed in the WordPerfect data-entry window?
11. What is a soft return? A hard return?
12. How do you move from one page to the next page?
13. How do you move from page 1 to page 24?
14. What is the function of the + sign in cursor movement? Of the − sign?
15. What does PgDn mean? PgUp?
*16. What is the default option when you are creating a document? What is the typeover option?
17. How do you insert two blank lines in a document?
18. How do you delete an entire line? An entire page? An entire paragraph?
*19. How do you save a WordPerfect document?
20. Why should you identify a drive or a directory when you save a file?
*21. How do you print a document?
22. How do you retrieve a saved file?
23. How do you generate a listing of your directory?
24. How do you delete an unwanted file?
25. How do you copy a file from one directory to another one?
26. How do you exit WordPerfect?
*27. When you exit, does WordPerfect automatically save your file?
28. How do you pull up the WordPerfect main menu using the keyboard? Using a mouse?
29. How many options are available in the main menu? How do you select a particular option?

HANDS-ON EXPERIENCE

1. Get WordPerfect started. Using the on-line help facility generate help for the Save and Exit commands.
2. Type the following document on your screen:

   > Using WordPerfect, numerous documents can be created. The nice feature about the program is its user-friendliness. Mistakes easily can be corrected.

   Do the following with this file:

   a. Replace "WordPerfect" with "a word processing program."

   b. Replace "mistakes" with "errors."

   c. Insert a blank line between lines 2 and 3.

   d. Save this file on your disk as EXCEL1.WP.

   e. Using the default options, print this document.

   f. How do you create a listing of the directory of your disk?
3. Type sections 3–2 through 3–4 as one document. Do the following with this file:

   a. Save your document as EXERCISE.

   b. Print the file.

c. Move the cursor to the beginning of the first page.
d. Move the cursor to the beginning of the last page.
e. Erase the first paragraph.
f. Move the cursor to the extreme right border of the document.
g. Try all the arrow-movement keys highlighted in table 3–1.
h. Try all the versions of the Delete command.
i. What is the application of each version of the Delete command?
j. Use F7 to erase the screen.
k. Retrieve the exercise document.
l. Add the following message to the end of your document:

   It is exciting to learn all these word processing features in this book. This knowledge should help me in writing reports and papers.

m. Save this document as PRACTICE.

4. Create a directory listing of the default drive. What are all the options under this command? Try to practice with all of these options.

KEY TERMS

Data-entry window
Dedicated word processor
Hard return
Keyboard template
Mainframe-based word processor
Merge
Microcomputer-based word processor
On-line help facility
Soft return
Speller
Status line
Thesaurus
Tutorial facility
Typeover
Word processor

KEY COMMANDS

Arrow movement commands (see table 3–1)
Delete commands (see table 3–2)
On-line help (F3)
Print (Shift-F7)
Retrieve (Shift-F10)
Save and Continue (F10)
Save and Exit (F7)
Undelete (F1)

MISCONCEPTIONS AND SOLUTIONS

Misconception After a WordPerfect session you may try to terminate the session by turning the computer off.

Solution This may damage segments of your program. Always exit the program by pressing F7, Yes to save your work and Yes to exit the program.

Misconception Pressing Backspace to erase a character generates unpredictable results.

Solution Backspace in Insert mode erases the characters to the left and closes the gap. In Typeover mode, the Backspace erases the characters to the left and inserts spaces.

Misconception Pressing the space bar to erase a character or to insert spaces creates unpredictable results.

Solution Check the mode first. In Typeover mode, the space bar erases the characters and leaves their place empty. In Insert mode it inserts spaces and moves the existing text to the right.

Misconception Pressing F5 displays all the files in your directory regardless of their types.

Solution Use wild cards to expedite the process. For example, B:*.WP will display only WordPerfect files in drive B.

DIFFERENCES BETWEEN WORDPERFECT 4.2 AND 5.0

- The minimum memory requirement of WordPerfect 4.2 is 256K.
- In WordPerfect 4.2, the position of the cursor is displayed in terms of spaces, not inches. For example:

```
Doc 1 Pg 1 Ln 1 Pos 10
```

- There are minor variations in figure 3–5.
- In WordPerfect 4.2 if you press Shift-F7 for the print menu you will see:

```
1 Full Text; 2 Page; 3 Options; 4 Printer Control; 5
Type-Thru; 6 Preview:0
```

- In WordPerfect 4.2, when you press F5 (Retrieve), the menu displayed is slightly different:

  Option 3 is Rename
  Option 7 is Change Directory
  The last option is Exit

DIFFERENCES BETWEEN WORDPERFECT 5.0 AND 5.1

- The minimum memory requirement of WordPerfect 5.0 is 384K.
- The on-line help facility in WordPerfect 5.0 is not context-sensitive.
- WordPerfect 5.0 does not provide mouse support or pull-down menus.
- WordPerfect 5.0 does not require a hard disk.
- There are slight differences in the print menus.
- When you press F5 in WordPerfect 5.0:

  Option 5 is Text In
  Option 9 is Word Search
  Option N(10) is Name Search

ARE YOU READY TO MOVE ON?

Multiple Choice

1. Using a word processor, you can

- **a.** create text
- **b.** edit the document
- **c.** do cut and paste
- **d.** all of the above
- **e.** none of the above

2. Which of the following is not a component of WordPerfect?

- **a.** spreadsheet (similar to Lotus 1-2-3)
- **b.** full feature word processor
- **c.** speller
- **d.** thesaurus
- **e.** all of the above

3. To start Wordperfect running from a hard disk, change the directory to the proper subdirectory (or use a modified path) and type
   a. WORD
   b. WP
   c. BEGIN
   d. START
   e. none of the above
4. The line at the bottom of the data-entry window is called the
   a. comment line
   b. command line
   c. status line
   d. memo line
   e. control line
5. Which function key is used to access the on-line help facility in WordPerfect?
   a. F1
   b. F8
   c. Shift-F7
   d. Alt-F8
   e. F3
6. The F1 (Cancel) key can be used to
   a. stop text from printing once the PRINT command has been given
   b. exit from WordPerfect
   c. undelete the last deletion if you change your mind
   d. all of the above
   e. none of the above
7. Which function key is used to save your file on the disk?
   a. F10
   b. Ctrl-F2
   c. F3
   d. F1
   e. Ctrl-F5
8. The template listing for the F7 key has the following layout:

   Footnote

   PRINT
   Columns/Table
   Exit

   To print a document using the F7 key, select
   a. F7
   b. Shift-F7
   c. Alt-F7
   d. Ctrl-F7
   e. Ctrl-Alt-F7

9. Each function key has more than one use because you can press the function key in combination with the
   a. Shift key
   b. Ctrl key
   c. Alt key
   d. all of the above
   e. none of the above
10. To delete an entire line, press
   a. Shift-Enter
   b. Ctrl-F2
   c. Ctrl-Enter
   d. Alt-PgDn
   e. Ctrl-End

True/False

1. Microcomputer-based word processors may possess some size and format limitations as compared to mainframe-based systems.
2. WordPerfect has only one major component, the word processor, while other programs include other components such as speller, thesaurus, and merge.
3. WordPerfect provides a context-sensitive help facility.
4. WordPerfect's standard display gives the cursor position in inches from the top margin and inches from the left margin.
5. When using WordPerfect, press the Enter key to create a soft return at the end of each line.
6. When using the arrow keys to move around the document, WordPerfect does not keep track of the cursor's relative position.
7. Pressing Home-Home-↑ will move the cursor to the beginning of the document.
8. When exiting WordPerfect, the program does not give you the option of saving your work.
9. Once you select the Exit option, you cannot stay in the program; you must exit to DOS.
10. To select an option from a WordPerfect menu, you can usually select the option number or the highlighted letter of the option.

ANSWERS

Multiple Choice

1. d
2. a
3. b
4. c
5. e
6. c
7. a
8. b
9. d
10. e

True/False

1. T
2. F
3. T
4. T
5. F
6. F
7. T
8. F
9. F
10. T

Formatting Text and Using the Spell Checker and Thesaurus

4

4–1 INTRODUCTION

In this chapter we present various commands for emphasizing text and changing the appearance of your reports. These commands include centering, underlining, boldfacing, case conversion, indenting, and justification. We discuss the speller and thesaurus features of WordPerfect, two features to help you generate more readable documents free of typographical errors.

4–2 INDENTING TEXT WITH THE TAB KEY

To indent a line, press the Tab key and start typing. To demonstrate this process, you will create a memo. First, start WordPerfect. The status line reads:

```
Doc 1    Pg 1    Ln 1"    Pos 1"
```

Press the Tab key, and Pos is changed to 1.5″. Now type the following memo, pressing the Tab and Enter keys as indicated:

From: Tom Morris, Personnel(Enter)
(Tab)
To: Administrative Staff(Enter)
(Enter)
Date: January 1, 1991
(Enter)
(Enter)
(Tab)
Subject: WordPerfect Seminar
(Enter)

```
     From: Tom Morris, Personnel
     To  : Administrative Staff
     Date: January 1, 1991

     Subject: WordPerfect Seminar

WordPerfect is one of the most popular word processing programs on
the market. The personnel office is planning to conduct a brief
seminar on this package.

Tom Morris from the personnel office will be the instructor. All
administrative staff are invited.

To encourage all of you to attend the seminar, there will be cash
prizes awarded to three of the participants.

After familiarizing yourselves with WordPerfect, all of you who
participate will be given access to a PC with WordPerfect
capabilities.



A:\WORDPB\CH4-1.WP                              Doc 1 Pg 1 Ln 1" Pos 1"
```

Figure 4–1
A Sample Memo

(Enter)
WordPerfect is one of the most popular word processing programs on the market. The personnel office is planning to conduct a brief seminar on this package.
(Enter)
(Enter)
Tom Morris from the personnel office will be the instructor. All administrative staff are invited.
(Enter)
(Enter)
To encourage all of you to attend the seminar, there will be cash prizes awarded to three of the participants.(Enter)
(Enter)
After familiarizing yourselves with WordPerfect, all of you who participate will be given access to a PC with WordPerfect capabilities.
(Enter)

At this point, your screen should be similar to the screen shown in figure 4–1. Save this screen by using the F10 function key, and name this file CH4-1.WP.

4–3 INDENTING TEXT WITH THE INDENT KEY

The temporary indent command (F4) resets the left margin to the next tab stop. The default tab stops occur every five spaces. This temporary indentation remains in effect until you press Enter.

4–4 CENTERING TEXT

Suppose that you are typing a brief report entitled "Sales Report for Western Regions." To **center** this title, press Shift-F6. The cursor is moved to the center of the first line. Now type the title.

4–5 UNDERLINING TEXT

To highlight the importance of a word or a series of words, you may want to **underline** them. Type the portion of a sales report presented in figure 4–2. Suppose that you want to underline the word "Western" in the first line. Move the cursor to the beginning of the word and do the following:

1. Turn the block feature on by pressing Alt-F4 or F12.
2. Highlight the word.
3. Press F8 (the Underline key).

To underline text while typing, press F8 and type the text to be underlined. To end underlining, press the F8 key again. You won't see the effect of the underline command on-screen; however, when you print the document, the word "Western" will be underlined. You can reveal the formatting codes by pressing Alt-F3 or F11. The word "Western" is preceded by [UND] and followed by [und]. If you don't want to keep the underline, you can reveal the code, and

Figure 4–2
A Portion of a Sales Report

SALES REPORT FOR WESTERN REGIONS
For the past three years western regions have demonstrated a significant increase in total sales. The major factor for this increase is due to the new advertising campaign.

then delete it using the Del key. To exit the Reveal Codes menu, press Alt-F3 again.

4–6 BOLDFACING TEXT

The **bold** feature highlights words in bold print. Various printers perform boldfacing differently, but usually by reprinting a word from two to six times. To make the phrase "past three years" bold in the sample sales report, do the following:

1. Move the cursor to the beginning of the phrase.
2. Turn the Block feature on (Alt-F4).
3. Highlight the words "past three years."
4. Press F6 (the Boldface key).

To make text bold while typing, press F6 and type your text. To end the bold option, press the F6 key again.

4–7 COMBINING COMMANDS

The bold and underline commands can be combined. To do this, you must turn on both features (it doesn't matter which feature is turned on first). Suppose that you want to boldface and underline the phrase "new advertising campaign." Do the following:

1. Move the cursor to the beginning of the phrase.
2. Turn on the Block feature (Alt-F4).
3. Highlight the phrase.
4. Press F6.
5. Move the cursor to the beginning of the phrase again.
6. Turn on the Block feature.
7. Highlight the phrase.
8. Press F8.

You can verify your work by revealing the codes (by pressing Alt-F3). The phrase "new advertising campaign" will be preceded by [BOLD][UND] and followed by [und][bold].

4–8 FLUSH RIGHT COMMAND

You can align text against the right margin with the Alt-F6 key combination. Suppose that you want to right-align the message "1990 has been a good year for all of us."

You do the following:

1. Move the cursor to the beginning of the line.
2. Turn on the Block feature (Alt-F4).
3. Highlight the message.
4. Press Alt-F6.

WordPerfect responds with:

```
[Just:Right]? No (Yes)
```

Press Y. You will see that your message is aligned against the right margin. This feature is mostly used to position headings, footings, dates, and special messages. You also can press Alt-F6 first, and then type your text.

4–9 LEFT-RIGHT INDENT

You use the Left-Right Indent command to indent both the left and right margins for a single paragraph. To do this, do the following:

1. Move the cursor to the beginning of the paragraph.
2. Press Shift-F4.

4–10 CASE CONVERSION COMMAND

For **case conversion** (to change a phrase from uppercase to lowercase or lowercase to uppercase), WordPerfect provides a simple command. Suppose that you want to change the title SALES REPORT FOR WESTERN REGIONS to lowercase. Do the following:

1. Move the cursor to the beginning of the message.
2. Turn on the Block feature (Alt-F4).
3. Highlight the message.
4. Press Shift-F3. The following menu is displayed:

```
1 Uppercase; 2 Lowercase: 0
```

5. From this menu select option 2.

4–11 TEXT JUSTIFICATION

WordPerfect 5.1 offers four types of **justification** to choose from. You can format your documents with left, center, right, or full justification, enabling you to arrange your text to fit your needs. To see this feature in action, start with a clear screen and follow these steps for left justification:

1. Press Shift-F8 (Format) to enter the Format menu.
2. Press 1 or L to enter the Format: Line menu.
3. Select 3 or J to enter the Justification menu.

4. For left justification, select 1 or L. This will give a ragged right margin to your printed output.
5. Press the space bar twice to return to document-editing mode.
6. Type the following text:

> Using left justification, your text will be aligned along the left margin and will have a flush left margin and a ragged right margin, as you can see in this example. You can see the effects of left justification on the screen and on the printed output.

> To see what center justification of text looks like, follow these steps:

1. Press Enter twice to insert two blank lines into the document.
2. Press Shift-F8 (Format) to enter the Format menu.
3. Press 1 or L to enter the Format: Line menu.
4. Select 3 or J to enter the Justification menu.
5. For center justification, select 2 or C. This will center your text between the left and right margins.
6. Press the space bar twice to return to document-editing mode.
7. Type the following text:

> Notice that when using center justification, your text is centered between the left and right margins. Both the left and right margins will be ragged. You can see the effect of center justification on the screen as well as the printed output.

> You also can right justify text. To do so, follow these steps:

1. Press Enter twice to insert two blank lines into the document.
2. Press Shift-F8 (Format) to enter the Format menu.
3. Press 1 or L to enter the Format: Line menu.
4. Select 3 or J to enter the Justification menu.
5. For right justification, select 3 or R. This will give a ragged left margin to your printed output.
6. Press the space bar twice to return to document-editing mode.
7. Type the following text:

> Notice that when you use right justification, the text appears on the right side of the screen as you type it, and is pushed to the left as more text is typed. This text is flush on the right side, and ragged on the left. You can see the effect of right justification on the screen as well as on the printed output.

You also can use full justification for your text. To fully justify your text, follow these steps:

1. Press Enter twice to insert two blank lines into the document.
2. Press Shift-F8 (Format) to enter the Format menu.
3. Press 1 or L to enter the Format: Line menu.

4. Select 3 or J to enter the Justification menu.
5. For full justification, select 4 or F. This gives flush margins on both the right and left sides.
6. Press the space bar twice to return to document-editing mode.
7. Type the following text:

> Full justification means that both the right and the left sides of the text will be flush with their respective margins. Note that you cannot see the effect of full justification on the screen, but you can see the effect in View Document mode and on the printed output.

Press Shift-F7 (Print) to enter the Print menu. Press 2 or P to print the page. Take a look at the effects of the various types of justification. Each has its own distinct appearance. Press F7 (Exit), N, N to clear the screen when you are finished working with justification.

4–12 THE SPELL CHECKER

The **spell checker** component of WordPerfect checks all the words in your document against a built-in dictionary or a supplemental dictionary you specify. If WordPerfect finds a misspelled word, it highlights the word. You can change it, leave it as it is, or add it to the dictionary. You can correct a word, a page, or the entire document. You also can change the dictionary. The word count option counts all the words in your document.

Different word processing programs have different spell checkers. The level of sophistication varies with the package. Be aware, however, that the spell checker cannot catch all mistakes. Many times a word is spelled correctly but it is used in the wrong context. For example, in the sentence, "Too students dropped the computer class," the word "too" is used incorrectly (misspelled), but it won't be highlighted by the spell checker.

4–13 STARTING THE SPELL CHECKER

The spell checker comes on a separate disk. You either must install this disk on your hard disk, or you must insert the disk into one of your drives. The document presented in figure 4–3 contains several obvious errors. To correct these misspelled words, do the following:

1. Press Ctrl-F2 to display the Spell Checker menu.
2. From this menu select option 3 for Document.

WordPerfect displays the first mistake, "aadminstrative," and suggests a correction. Press A to use this suggestion. Then, the next misspelled word, "sieminar," is displayed. This time WordPerfect suggests two replacements. Press A to choose option A as the replacement. The next misspelled word is "coduct." Again, press A to replace the incorrect word with the correct spelling. The next mistake is "offisce." Choose selection A to replace it. For the next error, "avarded," WordPerfect provides three suggestions. Choose option A. The last misspelling is "participte." Again, select option A. When you are finished, WordPerfect displays the following message:

```
Word count: 89    Press any key to continue
```

```
     From: Tom Morris, Personnel
     To  : Aadministrative Staff

     Subject: WordPerfect Sieminar

WordPerfect is one of the most popular word processing programs on
the market. The personnel office is planning to coduct a brief
seminar on this package.

Tom Morris from the personnel offisce will be the instructor. All
the administrative staff are invited.

To encourage all of you to attend the seminar, there will be cash
prizes avarded to three seminar participants.

After familiarizing yourselves with WordPerfect, all of who
participte will be given access to a PC with WordPerfect
capabilities.




A:\WORDPB\CH4-3.WP                              Doc 1 Pg 1 Ln 1" Pos 1"
```

Figure 4–3
A Sample Document with Misspellings

When two identical words, such as "is is," appear next to each other, WordPerfect automatically displays the Double Word menu. Select 3 (Delete 2nd) to eliminate the second word.

4–14 THE THESAURUS

The WordPerfect **thesaurus** displays a list of synonyms and antonyms for the word you indicate. The thesaurus contains about 15,000 words. The word you look up (the headword) is displayed on the screen border. The suggested replacement words are displayed as nouns (n), verbs (v), adjectives (a), and antonyms (ant).

4–15 STARTING THE THESAURUS

The thesaurus component of WordPerfect comes on a separate disk. You must install it on your hard disk or you must have this disk in one of your drives. On a blank screen, type the following:

In this chapter we explain the basics of word processing.

We want to know all the synonyms and antonyms of the word "explain." To use the thesaurus, do the following:

1. Move the cursor to any portion of the word "explain."
2. Press Alt-F1 to start the thesaurus. You see the screen shown in figure 4–4. As you can see, there are 12 synonyms and 1 antonym listed. Suppose that

```
In this chapter we will explain the basics of word processing.

explain=(v)
 1 A ·define
   B ·demonstrate
   C ·illustrate
   D ·interpret
   E ·resolve

 2 F ·decipher
   G ·illuminate
   H ·reveal
   I ·untangle

 3 J ·excuse
   K ·justify
   L ·rationalize

explain-(ant)
 4 M ·confuse

1 Replace Word; 2 View Doc; 3 Look Up Word; 4 Clear Column: 0
```

Figure 4–4
The Thesaurus Menu for the Word "Explain"

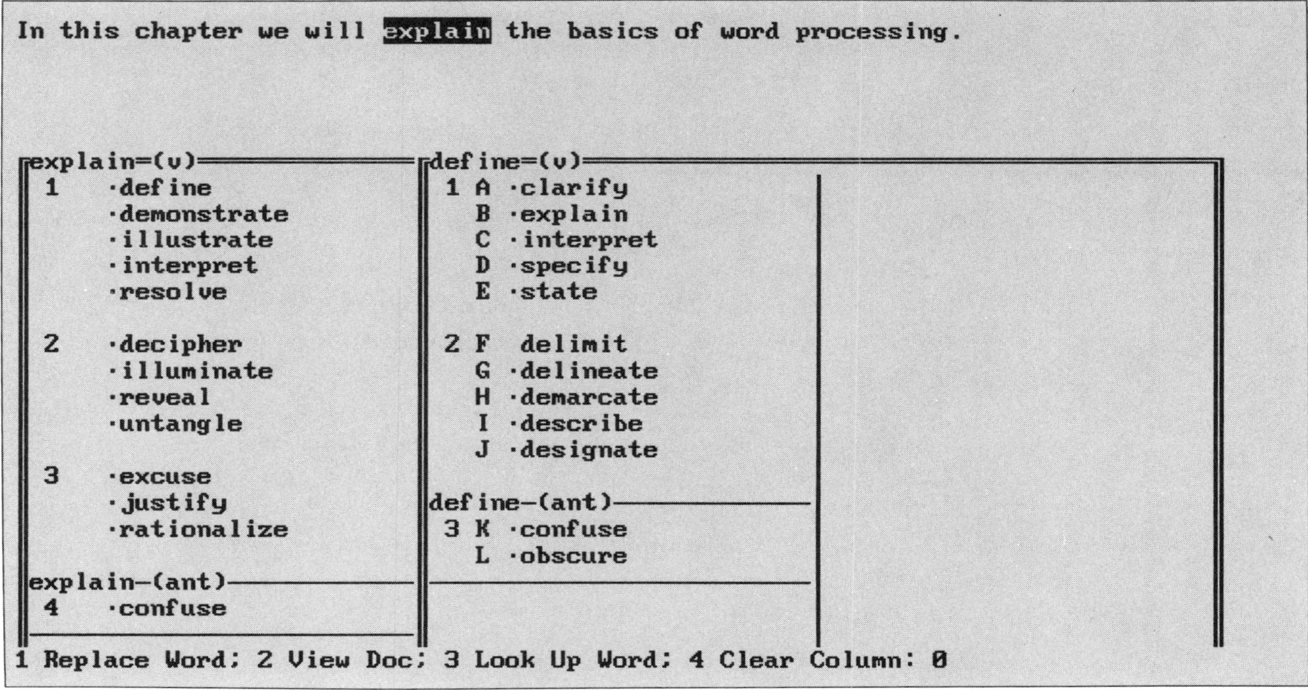

Figure 4–5
Additional Information for the Word "Define"

you need more information on one of these headwords, "define" for example. Press A. WordPerfect displays a second column, as shown in figure 4–5. You can access the words previously displayed in column 1 by pressing the left-arrow key.

3. If you don't need this additional information press 4 (Clear Column).
4. To replace "explain" with any of the words displayed in the additional column, select option 1 from the menu and press the letter for the desired word. To replace "explain" with "clarify," for example, select option 1 and press A. In a blink of an eye the word is replaced.

4–16 PULL-DOWN MENU HIGHLIGHTS

1. To justify text, move the cursor to where you want the text to be typed, and then from the main menu, select Layout and Justify. You can left-, center-, right-, or fully justify text. You also can first highlight the text, and then invoke the menu.
2. To indent, center, or make text flush right, put the cursor at the beginning of the text. From the main menu, select Layout and Align, and then select the desired option.
3. To start the spell checker, from the main menu select Tools and Spell. Select 1 for word, 2 for page, or 3 for document.
4. To start the thesaurus, position the cursor at the desired word, and then from the main menu select Tools and Thesaurus.

SUMMARY

This chapter introduced several commands for creating reports. The commands discussed are used for centering, boldfacing, case conversion, margin and justification. The chapter concluded with a discussion of the spell checker and thesaurus.

REVIEW QUESTIONS

*These questions are answered in Appendix A.

*1. How do you center a line?

2. How do you underline a word? A sentence?

3. Why might you boldface a word? How do you do this?

4. Can the Underline and Boldface commands be combined? Does one command take priority over the other?

*5. By looking at the screen, how do you know that a word is underlined? Boldfaced?

6. What is the flush right command? What are some applications of this command?

7. What are some applications of the Indent key? What is the difference between the Indent key and the Tab key?

8. What is left-right indent? How do you make a paragraph left and right indented?

*9. What is the case conversion command? Using this command, can all uppercase characters be replaced with lowercase characters?

10. What is the spell checker?

*11. How do you get the spell checker started?

12. Can you add a word to the WordPerfect dictionary?

13. What is the thesaurus?

14. How many words are included in WordPerfect's thesaurus?

*15. How do you get the thesaurus started?

16. How do you ask for more information on one of the choices displayed by the thesaurus?

HANDS-ON EXPERIENCE

1. Start WordPerfect. Begin with a blank screen and do the following:
   a. Center the following line:

      In 1992 our company will celebrate its 30th anniversary.

   b. Boldface 1992.
   c. Boldface and underline "its 30th."
   d. Make the following message flush right:

      It will be fun to go to Disneyland!

   e. Indent the following paragraph

      In the 50 years of their existence computers have grown beyond imagination. A $100 computer today has as much power as a million dollar computer of 50 years ago.

   f. Left-right indent the above paragraph.
   g. Convert "million dollar" to uppercase letters.
2. Type the word *companeon* on the screen, then start the spell checker. Find the right spelling for this word.
3. Start the thesaurus. Generate all the synonyms and antonyms for the word "glory." Choose the best replacement.
4. Retrieve the example document (EXERCISE) that you created in the last chapter. Do the following:
   a. Use the spell checker to find any mistakes in the document.
   b. Underline the first three lines of the document.
   c. Boldface the last three lines of the document.
   d. Boldface and underline the fifth line of the document.
   e. Flush right the last line of the document.
   f. Convert the first paragraph to all capital letters.

KEY TERMS

Bold
Case conversion
Center
Justification
Spell checker
Thesaurus
Underline

KEY COMMANDS

To start the thesaurus (Alt-F1)
Reveal Codes (Alt-F3)
To turn on the Block feature (Alt-F4)
Flush Right command (Alt-F6)
To start the spell checker (Ctrl-F2)
Cancel (F1)
Indent (F4)
Boldface (F6)
Exit (F7)
Underline (F8)
Case Conversion command (Shift-F3)
Left-Right Indent (Shift-F4)
To center the text (Shift-F6)

DIFFERENCES BETWEEN WORDPERFECT 4.2 AND 5.0

- The message for the flush right command in WordPerfect 4.2 is

```
[AlnFlshr] (Y/N) N
```

DIFFERENCES BETWEEN WORDPERFECT 5.0 AND 5.1

- The message for the flush right command in WordPerfect 5.0 is

```
[FlshRt]?(Y/N) No
```

ARE YOU READY TO MOVE ON?

Multiple Choice

1. To begin centering text, press
   a. F7
   b. Alt-F2
   c. Shift-F6
   d. F10
   e. F5
2. To underline text, press
   a. F8
   b. F10
   c. Shift-F1
   d. Shift-F5
   e. Shift-F7
3. "Flush right" means
   a. text is aligned against the left margin
   b. text is aligned against the right margin
   c. text is centered on the line
   d. text is centered on the page
   e. text has passed the spell check
4. The Shift-F4 key is used to
   a. start a new paragraph, similar to the Tab key
   b. insert a hard page break
   c. indent the left margin only
   d. indent both the left and right margins
   e. underline the text
5. The command to change from lowercase to uppercase (or vice versa) is part of the function
   a. Ctrl-F1
   b. Ctrl-F2
   c. Shift-F1
   d. Shift-F2
   e. Shift-F3

6. After the spell checker has identified a potentially misspelled word, you have the option to
   a. replace it with one of the choices provided
   b. skip the word, leaving it in its current form
   c. add the word to your personal dictionary
   d. edit the word yourself
   e. all of the above
7. To count the number of words in a document, use the command
   a. Setup (Shift-F1)
   b. Search (F2)
   c. Spell (Ctrl-F2)
   d. Mark Text (Alt-F5)
   e. Format (Shift-F8)
8. The F4 key is used to
   a. start a new paragraph, similar to the Tab key
   b. insert a hard page break
   c. indent the left margin only
   d. indent both the left and right margins
   e. underline the text
9. To find a substitute word to make your document more meaningful and readable, you would probably choose the
   a. thesaurus
   b. spell checker
   c. Replace feature
   d. Switch feature
   e. none of the above
10. WordPerfect's default tab stops are every
    a. 10 spaces
    b. 5 spaces
    c. 15 spaces
    d. 1 space
    e. none of the above

True/False

1. The Tab key can be used to indent a line.
2. To underline text that you have already typed, you must first block the text before pressing F8.
3. You cannot boldface text you have already typed; you must delete it first and press F6 before typing the text.
4. Boldface and underline commands cannot be combined.
5. The flush right function is accessed by pressing Alt-F6.
6. To indent only the left margin two tab stops, press F4 twice.
7. The spell checker will find all spelling and grammar mistakes.
8. The thesaurus suggests only synonyms (same meaning); it does not suggest antonyms (opposite meaning).

9. When the Caps Lock key is activated, the cursor position indicator appears as POS.
10. Some monitors cannot display a true underline; therefore, there is no way to determine if your text is underlined without printing it.

ANSWERS

Multiple Choice

1. c
2. a
3. b
4. d
5. e
6. e
7. c
8. c
9. a
10. b

True/False

1. T
2. T
3. F
4. F
5. T
6. T
7. F
8. F
9. T
10. F

5

Search and Replace Operations, WordPerfect Codes, and Working with Blocks of Data

5–1

INTRODUCTION

In this chapter, the process of searching and replacing text will be explained. Formatting codes and their importance in creating specific documents will be discussed. The tab ruler and windows, which allow you to view two documents at the same time, will be examined. The chapter concludes with a discussion on working with blocks of data. Cut, Move, and Delete operations using blocks will also be reviewed.

5–2

SEARCHING AND REPLACING TEXT

Many times you want to replace a word or a series of words with a new word or series. WordPerfect can replace any word or phrase with another word or phrase. The length does not matter. To show how the **search and replace** feature works, suppose that Tom Morris was just notified that he must go to Europe. Bob Brown has been asked to take his place. In the memo shown in figure 5–1, you want to to replace the name "Tom Morris" with "Bob Brown."

Move to the top of the memo, and enter WordPerfect's search facility by pressing Alt-F2. WordPerfect responds:

```
w/Confirm? No (Yes)
```

It is asking you if you would like to confirm (approve) each replacement. Press Enter to indicate no. WordPerfect responds:

```
-->Srch:
```

WordPerfect is asking you what you are searching for. Type *Tom Morris* and press F2 (the search key). WordPerfect responds:

```
Replace with:
```

Type *Bob Brown* and press F2. In a blink of an eye, the two occurrences of "Tom Morris" are replaced with "Bob Brown." The cursor sits at the last occurrence of the replaced text.

If you respond yes to the confirmation prompt, WordPerfect finds and stops at each occurrence of the specified text. WordPerfect prompts

```
Confirm? No (Yes)
```

If you answer Y, it replaces the text and continues to the next occurrence of the text (if there is any). If you respond N, it does not replace the word and continues to the next occurrence of the text (if there is any) and the process continues.

5–3

FORMATTING CODES

When you generate a document, WordPerfect adds special invisible **formatting codes** to your document. Although you do not see these codes, WordPerfect keeps track of them internally. These formatting codes are essential when you are trying to change the appearance of your document.

```
     From: Tom Morris, Personnel
     To  : Administrative Staff

     Subject: WordPerfect Seminar

WordPerfect is one of the most popular word processing programs on
the market. The personnel office is planning to conduct a brief
seminar on this package.

Tom Morris from the personnel office will be the instructor. All
administrative staff are invited.

To encourage all of you to attend the seminar, there will be cash
prizes awarded to three of the participants.

After familiarizing yourselves with WordPerfect, all of you who
participate will be given access to a PC with WordPerfect
capabilities.




A:\WORDPB\CH5-1.WP                              Doc 1 Pg 1 Ln 3.17" Pos 6.3"
```

Figure 5–1
A Sample Document

Suppose that in figure 5–1, you want to combine paragraphs 1 and 2. To do so, you must get rid of certain invisible codes. Move the cursor to the blank line between the two paragraphs. To reveal the formatting codes, press Alt-F3 (or F11 on extended keyboards). Your screen will be split into two horizontal sections (see fig. 5–2). The screens are separated by a **tab ruler.** (Tabs are represented by solid triangles, and the margin is represented by a brace.) The cursor is in the same position in both screens. As you see in the lower screen, the **soft return** is represented by [SRt] and the **hard return** by [HRt]. To connect the two paragraphs, you must eliminate both hard returns. Press Del to delete the HRt on the line between paragraphs. Then move the cursor to the hard return in the first paragraph and press Del. The two paragraphs will be connected (see fig. 5–3). To leave the formatting codes screen, press Alt-F3 or F11 again. Now your memo includes only three paragraphs.

Other commonly used codes include [CENTER] or [C/A/Flrt] for centering text, [BOLD] or [bold] for boldfacing text, and [UND] or [und] for underlining text.

5–4 SPLITTING A PARAGRAPH

To split the first paragraph shown in figure 5–1 into two, move the cursor to the beginning of the sentence that will become the new paragraph (The). Press Enter twice. The first Enter splits the two lines and the second Enter inserts a blank line. To rejoin the split paragraphs, move the cursor to the right of the first sentence. Press Del twice. You may have to use the space bar to insert blank spaces between the two sentences.

```
     From: Tom Morris, Personnel
     To  : Administrative Staff

     Subject: WordPerfect Seminar

WordPerfect is one of the most popular word processing programs on
the market. The personnel office is planning to conduct a brief
seminar on this package.

Tom Morris from the personnel office will be the instructor. All
administrative staff are invited.

To encourage all of you to attend the seminar, there will be cash
A:\WORDPB\CH5-1.WP                              Doc 1 Pg 1 Ln 2.33" POS 3.4"
{    ▲    ▲    ▲    ▲    ▲    ▲    ▲    ▲    ▲    ▲    ▲    ▲    }    ▲    ▲
the market. The personnel office is planning to conduct a brief[SRt]
seminar on this package.[HRt]
[HRt]
Tom Morris from the personnel office will be the instructor. All [SRt]
administrative staff are invited.[HRt]
[HRt]
To encourage all of you to attend the seminar, there will be cash[SRt]

Press Reveal Codes to restore screen
```

Figure 5–2
Formatting Codes for Figure 5–1

```
     From: Tom Morris, Personnel
     To  : Administrative Staff

     Subject: WordPerfect Seminar

WordPerfect is one of the most popular word processing programs on
the market. The personnel office is planning to conduct a brief
seminar on this package. Tom Morris from the personnel office will
be the instructor. All administrative staff are invited.

To encourage all of you to attend the seminar, there will be cash
prizes awarded to three of the participants.

After familiarizing yourselves with WordPerfect, all of you who
participate will be given access to a PC with WordPerfect
capabilities.




A:\WORDPB\CH5-3.WP                              Doc 1 Pg 1 Ln 2.5" Pos 5.5"
```

Figure 5–3
The First Two Paragraphs of Figure 5–1 Are Connected

5–5 DISPLAYING THE TAB RULER

The tab ruler displays margins and tab stops. It displays different information while you are moving through the document. On the tab ruler, a solid triangle indicates a tab stop, brackets indicate the left and right margins, and a brace indicates a left or right margin and a tab stop in the same location. To display the tab ruler follow these steps:

1. Press Ctrl-F3 to display the menu.
2. From this menu, select option 1 to get into the window. WordPerfect responds:

```
Number of lines in this window: 24
```

3. Press the up-arrow key one time to display the tab ruler at the bottom of the screen. Now you will see the triangles, brackets, and braces.
4. Press the down-arrow key one time to remove the tab ruler. The screen should still show the message:

```
Number of lines in this window: 24
```

5. Press Enter to return to the document.

5–6 USING WINDOWS

WordPerfect enables you to display and edit two documents at the same time. To do so, you must first display the Tab Ruler menu (Ctrl-F3). Choose option 1, then when the system asks you

```
Number of lines in this window: 24
```

enter *12* and press Enter to split the screen in half.

You can display a document on each side of the tab ruler. If the solid triangles are pointing up, the cursor is in the first document. If the solid triangles are pointing down, the cursor is in the second document. To move the cursor between the two windows (documents) use Shift-F3. You can retrieve a second document in the other window with Shift-F10. The document will appear below the tab ruler and the triangles will point downward.

To return to a single screen, press Ctrl-F3, 1, and in response to the prompt

```
Number of lines in this window:
```

type *24* and press Enter. If you are in document 2, the status line displays

```
Doc 2
```

To get into document 1, press Shift-F3. This feature can be very helpful for viewing two documents at the same time. You may want to compare and contrast two documents, or you may want to cut a section of one document and paste it into the other document.

5–7 MODIFYING STANDARD TABS AND MARGINS

So far we have been using the predefined tabs and margins (the default values of WordPerfect). You can create different kinds of tabs and margins using WordPerfect formatting features. Figure 5–4 shows a portion of the report that we want to create using WordPerfect.

We want to set up two columns: one for region and one for total sales. To change the tab settings, press Shift-F8. The menu shown in figure 5–5 is presented. If you choose option 1 from this menu, the menu shown in figure 5–6 is displayed. If you select option 8 from this menu, the menu shown in figure 5–7 is displayed.

Each L represents one tab stop on the ruler line. As you can see, every five positions there is a tab stop identified by the letter L. The options on the Tab Set menu include the following:

1. Delete EOL (Ctrl-End) clears all tabs.
2. Enter Number sets tabs at a specific interval.
3. Del clears one tab position.
4. Type sets relative or absolute tabs. Relative tabs adjust automatically to left and right margin changes. Absolute tabs do not adjust.
5. Left; Center; Right; Decimal. You can use these options for left justification, centering, right justification, or to establish decimal tabs that will line up numbers around the decimal point.
6. Dot Leader is used to make dot leadered tabs (as in a Table of Contents).
7. Exit (F7) is used to leave the menu.

Move the cursor to the left margin by pressing Home and the left-arrow key. Next, press Ctrl-End to erase all the tabs. At this point, the ruler line is represented by a series of dots. You can either cancel the tab operation and return to your document by pressing F1, or you can establish new tab settings. To create new tabs, you first must enter the tab type. Press T for type. WordPerfect responds with:

```
Tab Type: 1 Absolute; 2 Relative to Margin: 0
```

Relative tabs adjust automatically to any left or right margin changes and are called dynamic tabs. Absolute tab stops are static and do not adjust to accommodate margin changes. Select A for absolute, and then type *2.5* and press Enter.

Figure 5–4
A Portion of a Financial Report

Sales Report for Western Regions

For the past three years western regions have demonstrated a significant increase in total sales. The major factor for this increase is the new advertising campaign. The following are the selected regions:

Region	Total Sales (In Thousands)
Los Angeles	696,272.18
Portland	11,121.65
San Diego	28,169.22
Seattle	9,171.82

```
Format

     1 - Line
              Hyphenation                       Line Spacing
              Justification                     Margins Left/Right
              Line Height                       Tab Set
              Line Numbering                    Widow/Orphan Protection

     2 - Page
              Center Page (top to bottom)       Page Numbering
              Force Odd/Even Page               Paper Size/Type
              Headers and Footers               Suppress
              Margins Top/Bottom

     3 - Document
              Display Pitch                     Redline Method
              Initial Codes/Font                Summary

     4 - Other
              Advance                           Overstrike
              Conditional End of Page           Printer Functions
              Decimal Characters                Underline Spaces/Tabs
              Language

Selection: 0
```

Figure 5–5
The Format Menu

WordPerfect displays the letter L in position 2.5″, which indicates the tab position. Set a second tab by typing *5* and pressing Enter. Now you can go to the blank screen by pressing Exit (F7). Press Enter twice. Now you are ready to type the sales region data. Type the title of the report as centered (Shift-F6) and skip a line (Enter). Type the next two lines and skip a line. Press Tab and the cursor

```
Format: Line

     1 - Hyphenation                        No

     2 - Hyphenation Zone - Left            10%
                            Right           4%

     3 - Justification                      Full

     4 - Line Height                        Auto

     5 - Line Numbering                     No

     6 - Line Spacing                       1

     7 - Margins - Left                     1"
                   Right                    1"

     8 - Tab Set                            Rel: -1", every 0.5"

     9 - Widow/Orphan Protection            No


Selection: 0
```

Figure 5–6
The Format: Line Menu

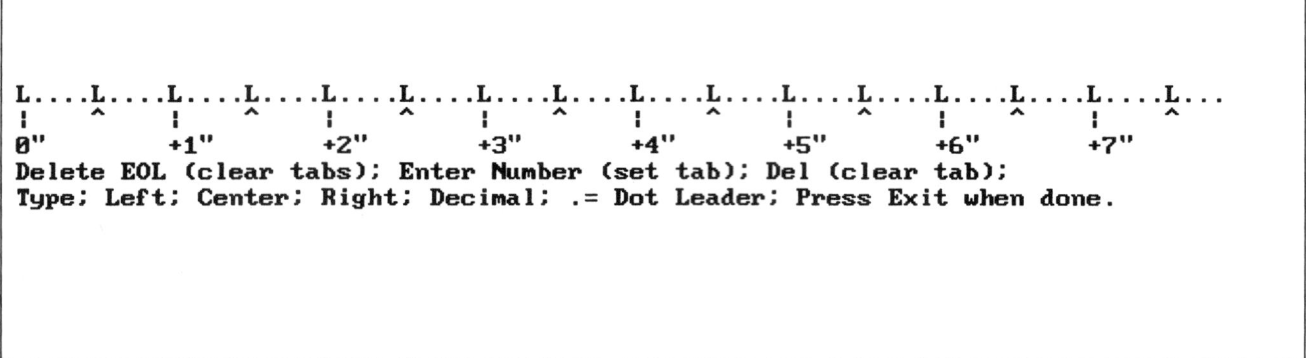

Figure 5–7
The Tab Set Menu

jumps to position 2.5″ (the first tab stop). Type region and press the Tab key again. The cursor jumps to position 5″ (the second tab stop). Type the rest of the data. At this point, your report should look like the one in figure 5–8.

As you can see, the numbers are not lined up. They are aligned from the left, but you want to align numbers around the decimal point. To do so, follow these steps:

1. Reveal formatting codes (press Alt-F3).
2. Position the cursor immediately after the tab set code, then press Shift-F8. (The cursor in the upper window must be in the same line as "Region" is.)
3. Choose options 1 and then 8.

```
                  Sales Report for Western Regions

For the past three years western regions have demonstrated a
significant increase in total sales. The major factor for this
increase is the new advertising campaign. The following are the
selected regions:

                 Region                 Total Sales(in thousands)
               ===========              ==========================
               Los Angeles              696,272.18
               Portland                 11,121.65
               San Diego                28,169.22
               Seattle                  9,171.82

A:\WORDPB\CH5-8.WP                                Doc 1 Pg 1 Ln 1" Pos 1"
```

Figure 5–8
A Report with Two Tab Settings

```
                Sales Report for Western Regions

For the past three years western regions have demonstrated a
significant increase in total sales. The major factor for this
increase is the new advertising campaign. The following are the
selected regions:

                  Region                    Total Sales(in thousands)
                ===========                 ========================
                Los Angeles                  696,272.18
                Portland                      11,121.65
                San Diego                     28,169.22
                Seattle                        9,171.82

A:\WORDPB\CH5-9.WP                                 Doc 1 Pg 1 Ln 1" Pos 1"
```

Figure 5–9
Aligning Numbers Around the Decimal Point

4. Position the cursor at location 6″ and type *D* (for decimal).
5. Press F7, and then press Enter twice to exit to the document.
6. Turn the Reveal Codes feature off (Alt-F3).
7. Press the down arrow twice and press Ctrl-right arrow three times to position the cursor at the beginning of the first number.
8. Press the Tab key, then the left-arrow key and the down-arrow key.
9. Repeat step 8 three times. As you can see in figure 5–9, the numbers are aligned around the decimal point.

Another important option in the Line menu is Line Spacing (option 6). By default, WordPerfect prints single-spaced documents. To change this format, retrieve your document and move the cursor to where you want to start the double-spaced format. Press Shift-F8 and select options 1 and then 6. Type *2* and press Enter three times to accept double-spacing and return to the document. Your document will be double-spaced beginning from the point where the cursor was placed.

5–8 INSERTING THE DATE AND TIME

You can always type the date and time as text in your document. However, if you do this, the date and time text is static. This means that it will not change when you retrieve this file later. You can also enter the static date from a menu. To do so, follow these steps:

1. Press Shift-F5 to display the Date menu.
2. Select Date Text (option 1).

The current system date will be inserted at the cursor position.

However, WordPerfect contains a function option that makes the date and time dynamic. For example, suppose that you want to insert the correct time and date on the top of the report presented in figure 5–10. Follows these steps:

1. Move the cursor to the top of the report.
2. Press Enter twice to insert two blank lines.
3. Move the cursor to the first blank line.
4. Press Shift-F5 to display the Date menu.
5. From this menu select 2 (Date Code).

The current system date will be displayed on the blank line. When the document is retrieved, the date will be the system date. To display the current time, press Enter to move the cursor to the second blank line and follow these steps:

1. Press Shift-F5 to get to the Date menu.
2. From this menu select option 3 (Date Format). The date format menu is displayed.
3. At the Date Format prompt, which reads

   ```
   3 1, 4
   ```

   type *8:90* to change the format to hours and minutes.
4. Press Enter to return to the Date menu.
5. Select 2 (Date Code).

```
January 1, 1991
9:28 AM

                Sales Report for Western Regions

For the past three years western regions have demonstrated a
significant increase in total sales. The major factor for this
increase is the new advertising campaign.

                 Region                 Total Sales(in thousands)
               ===========              =========================
               Los Angeles               696,272.18
               Portland                   11,121.65
               San Diego                  28,169.22
               Seattle                     9,171.82

A:\WORDPB\CH5-10.WP                                 Doc 1 Pg 1 Ln 1" Pos 1"
```

Figure 5–10
A Report with Date and Time

The current time is displayed below the date. If you change the date and time of your system at the DOS prompt and retrieve your document, the new date and time will be displayed in the document.

5–9 WORKING WITH BLOCKS OF DATA

The majority of word processing programs handle documents as **blocks of data.** A block can be a character, a word, a series of words, a paragraph, a series of paragraphs, or the entire document. With WordPerfect, you must define the block first, and then issue the appropriate command. To work with a block of data, do the following:

1. Move the cursor to the beginning of the data you want to alter.
2. Press Alt-F4 (or F12) to turn on the Block feature. (To turn it off, press Alt-F4 again.) At this point the status line flashes

```
Block on
```

3. Highlight a desired block by using the arrow keys. The highlighted data always stands out. On color monitors, the highlighted data is in a different color.
4. You can enter codes at the beginning and end of a block or simply issue the command.

WordPerfect handles three types of blocks: lines, columns, and rectangles. A line runs from the beginning of a sentence to the end of the sentence. Columns are identified by tab stops, indents, hard carriage returns, or tab aligns. Rectangles are blocks of data containing rows and columns. You can perform the Move, Copy, Delete, and Append operations on blocks of data.

To make this discussion more clear, in a blank screen create a document like the one in figure 5–11 by following these steps:

1. Move the cursor to the top of the screen and type *Div 1*. Press the Tab key to move to the next tab stop.
2. Type *10, 20, 30,* and *40,* pressing Tab after each number.
3. Press Enter.
4. Type *Div 2* and press the Tab key.
5. Type *50, 60, 70,* and *80,* pressing Tab after each number.
6. Press Enter.
7. Type *Div 3* and press Tab.
8. Type *90, 100, 110,* and *120,* pressing Tab after each number.

Suppose that you want to move the second column to column 6. Do the following:

1. Move the cursor to the beginning of the second column (number 10).
2. Turn on the Block feature (Alt-F4). At this point, "Block on" is flashing on the status line.
3. Highlight the entire column. Don't panic—some other areas are highlighted when you press the down-arrow key.

```
Div 1      10    20    30    40
Div 2      50    60    70    80
Div 3      90    100   110   120




A:\WORDPB\CH5-11.WP                          Doc 1 Pg 1 Ln 1" Pos 1"
```

Figure 5–11
A Sample Document

4. Press Ctrl-F4 to display the Block Move menu.
5. From this menu, select option C (or 2) for Column. A new menu is presented:

```
1 Move; 2 Copy; 3 Delete; 4 Append: 0
```

6. From this menu, select 1.

The old second column has been cut and stored in the buffer and the table is closed up. The table now includes four columns. To move the original column 1 to the end of the table, move the cursor to the right of the number 40. WordPerfect displays

```
Move cursor; press Enter to retrieve
```

Press Enter. You will see:

```
Div 1        20       30       40       10
Div 2        60       70       80       50
Div 3       100      110      120       90
```

5–10

MOVING TEXT (CUT AND PASTE)

Cut and paste operations apply to tables as well as to regular text. WordPerfect enables you to move any portion of a document from one location to another.

Suppose that in figure 5–1, you want to move the second paragraph to the end of the memo. Move the cursor to the beginning of the second paragraph and press Alt-F4 or F12 to turn on the Block feature. Highlight the area you want to move. Press Ctrl-F4. The following menu is presented:

```
     From: Tom Morris, Personnel
     To  : Administrative Staff

     Subject: WordPerfect Seminar

WordPerfect is one of the most popular word processing programs on
the market. The personnel office is planning to conduct a brief
seminar on this package.



To encourage all of you to attend the seminar, there will be cash
prizes awarded to three of the participants.

After familiarizing yourselves with WordPerfect, all of you who
participate will be given access to a PC with WordPerfect
capabilities.

Tom Morris from the personnel office will be the instructor. All
administrative staff are invited .


A:\WORDPB\CH5-12.WP                          Doc 1 Pg 1 Ln 1" Pos 1"
```

Figure 5–12
Moving Paragraphs

```
Move: 1 Block; 2 Tabular Column; 3 Rectangle: 0
```

Select 1 to choose Block. Next, WordPerfect displays the following menu:

```
1 Move; 2 Copy; 3 Delete; 4 Append: 0
```

Choose 1 for Move. Move the cursor to the end of the memo. The status line displays:

```
Move cursor; press Enter to retrieve
```

Press Enter. You have successfully moved the paragraph (see fig. 5–12). To skip a line between the last two paragraphs, you should press Enter.

5–11 DELETING BLOCKS OF TEXT

Suppose that you want to delete the second paragraph in figure 5–1. Move the cursor to the beginning of the paragraph and press Alt-F4. The status line flashes

```
Block on
```

Use the down-arrow key to highlight the area that you intend to delete. Press the Del key. WordPerfect responds:

```
Delete Block? No(Yes)
```

Press Y and the block disappears. If you change your mind, the undelete feature enables you to restore the deleted text. You can undelete the text by pressing the F1 function key. The most recently deleted paragraph is highlighted and the following menu is displayed:

```
Undelete: 1 Restore; 2 Previous Deletion: 0
```

Press 1 to restore the deleted paragraph. To highlight and restore the previous deletions, select option 2 from this menu. Note that only the most recent deletion and the two previous deletions may be recalled in this manner. The portion of the text stored in the undo buffer can be restored to any place in the document, not just the area from which it was initially deleted.

5–12 PULL-DOWN MENU HIGHLIGHTS

1. To do search and replace operations, from the main menu select Search. Then choose Forward, Backward, Next, Previous, or Replace.
2. To reveal formatting codes, from the main menu select Edit and Reveal Codes.
3. To display the tab ruler, select Edit from the main menu, and then select Window. Press the up arrow, and then press Enter to see the tab ruler.
4. To create two windows, from the main menu select Edit, and then select Window. Type *12* and press Enter.
5. To set tabs, select Layout from the main menu, and then select Line. Choose option 8, Tab Set.
6. To insert the date into your document, choose Tools from the main menu, and then select Date Code.
7. To establish a block of text, from the main menu choose Edit, and then select Block. Move the cursor to the end of the area to be blocked.
8. To move (cut), copy, paste, append, or delete text, from the main menu select Edit and the desired option. Text must have been blocked first.

SUMMARY

In this chapter we discussed search and replace operations. Displaying and using the tab ruler and windows were highlighted. We discussed joining and splitting paragraphs. You learned how to insert the date and time using WordPerfect functions. We explained how to use the Block feature with the Move, Cut, Copy, and Delete operations, and you learned about WordPerfect's undelete feature.

REVIEW QUESTIONS

*These questions are answered in Appendix A.

1. How do you get the search process started?
2. How do you tell WordPerfect to replace a word with another word?
*3. In search and replace operations, are the two words (original and replacement) supposed to be of equal length?
4. What is the confirmation process? Can you bypass this step?
5. What are formatting codes?
*6. How do you reveal the formatting codes?

7. How do you display the tab ruler?
8. What is the role of solid triangles on the tab ruler?
9. What are windows?
10. How do you create windows?
*11. How do you move between the two windows?
12. Does the direction of the solid triangle tell you about the position of the cursor?
13. How do you modify the standard tabs and margins?
14. Why might you want to reset the standard tabs?
*15. How do you erase the standard tabs?
16. What character is used to make a new tab?
17. What character illustrates that the new tab is established?
18. How do you insert the dynamic date and time into your document?
19. What is the difference between using this function versus typing the date and time directly as text?
20. What is a block of data?
21. How do you turn on the Block feature? How do you turn it off?
22. What are some of the operations that can be performed on blocks of data?
23. How do you move a column of a table to another column of the same table?
*24. What are the applications of the Cut command?
25. How do you delete a block of data?
*26. Can you change your mind after deleting a block? How do you restore the deleted text?

HANDS-ON EXPERIENCE

1. Using figure 5–1 do the following:
   a. Add the following paragraph to the text:

      After the WordPerfect seminar, the personnel office is planning to conduct a Lotus 1-2-3 seminar.

   b. Indent the first line of this paragraph.
   c. Replace "WordPerfect" with "Wordstar."
   d. Replace all occurrences of "M" with "N."
   e. Change all occurrences of "N" back to "M."
   f. Join the fourth and fifth paragraphs.
   g. Split the first paragraph into two paragraphs.
   h. Display the tab ruler.
   i. Move the cursor back and forth between the two screens.
2. Create the following table:

Quarter 1	Quarter 2	Quarter 3
10	40	70
20	50	80
30	60	90

   a. Copy Quarter 1 after Quarter 3.
   b. Cut Quarter 1 and paste it after Quarter 3.

3. In figure 5–1, by using the Block feature, cut the first paragraph and paste it at the end of the text.
4. In figure 5–1, by using the Block feature, delete the second paragraph. Use the Undo feature to restore the paragraph.
5. Set tabs in columns 1.5″, 3″, 4.5″, and 6″. Do the following:
   a. Right-justify column 1.5″.
   b. Center column 3.0″.
   c. Left-justify column 4.5″.
   d. Decimal align column 6.0″. Enter the following data in these columns:

Portland	200	66	22.91
Los Angeles	92	796	121.52
London	500	12	1.16

   Notice how your data is presented on-screen.
6. Using the date function, insert the date and time in your previous screen.
7. Retrieve the EXERCISE document as Doc 1. Retrieve the PRACTICE document as Doc 2 in the second window. (You created these documents in Chapter 15.) Do the following:
   a. Copy the last paragraph of Doc 2 and paste it to the end of Doc 1.
   b. Exit to Doc 1.
   c. Replace all occurrences of "the" with "xxx."
   d. Replace all occurrences of "xxx" with "the."
   e. Insert the system date and time at the top of this document.
   f. Delete the first paragraph.

KEY TERMS

Block of data
Cut and paste
Formatting codes
Hard return
Search and replace
Soft return
Tab ruler

KEY COMMANDS

Start the search operation (Alt-F2)

Reveal the formatting codes (Alt-F3)

Turn on the Block feature (Alt-F4)

Display the tab ruler (Ctrl-F3)

Display the Block Move menu (Ctrl-F4)

Delete a character or a block (Del)

Search key (F2)

Save a file (F10)

Move the cursor between the two windows (Shift-F3)

Display the date menu (Shift-F5)

Move the cursor five positions (Tab)

MISCONCEPTIONS AND SOLUTIONS

Misconception You turn the Block feature on and change your mind.

Solution Turn it off by pressing Alt-F4 or press F1.

Misconception You try to justify a line or paragraph and you don't get the correct result.

Solution You can justify only if the line or paragraph is ended by a hard carriage return. Enter the return first, and then try to justify the text.

Misconception The only way to see the final appearance of your text is to reveal the format codes, which is time-consuming.

> **Solution** A faster method is to move the cursor to the desired text and look at the number following Pos in the status line. If the text is underlined, this number is underlined. If text is bold, this number is bold, and so on.

DIFFERENCES BETWEEN WORDPERFECT 4.2 AND 5.0

- In WordPerfect 4.2, codes for centering, boldfacing, and underlining are

  [C] or [c] for centering text
  [B] or [b] for boldfacing text
  [U] or [u] for underlining text

- In WordPerfect 4.2, you press Ctrl-F4 to display the Block Move menu. From this menu select 4 for Cut/Copy Column. After this a menu will be displayed that is slightly different from WordPerfect 5.0. This menu includes only three options:

```
1 Cut; 2 Copy; 3 Delete: 0
```

- To move a column in WordPerfect 4.2, after highlighting the column you must:

  1. Press Ctrl-F4 to display the Move menu.
  2. From this menu you must select option 4 for Column. As you noticed this process is one step shorter in WordPerfect 5.0.

- In WordPerfect 4.2 when you press Ctrl-F4, the following menu is displayed:

```
1 Cut Block; 2 Copy Block; 3 Append; 4 Cut/Copy Column; 5 Cut/Copy Rectangle
```

- In WordPerfect 4.2 when you press Shift-F8 for tab setting, you see the following menu:

```
1 2 Tabs; 3 Margins; 4 Spacing; 5 Hyphenation; 6 Align Char: 0
```

  From this menu you can select either option 1 or option 2 to see figure 5–7.

- In WordPerfect 4.2 to insert the date and time into your document you first press Shift-F5 then you must select Insert Text. This will insert the system date into your document. To insert the system time into your document, first press Shift-F5 then select 3 (Insert Function).

DIFFERENCES BETWEEN WORDPERFECT 5.0 AND 5.1

- In WordPerfect 5.0, when you press Ctrl-F4 you see the following menu:

```
1 Move; 2 Copy; 3 Delete; 4 Append: 0
```

- The Shift-F8 menu in WordPerfect 5.0 is slightly different from 5.1.

- With WordPerfect 5.0, text can be left or right justified. With release 5.1, text can be left, full (right), or center justified.
- Using WordPerfect 5.1, tab stops can be set to relative or absolute, and existing tab stops can be adjusted to new settings, carrying the text with them.

ARE YOU READY TO MOVE ON?

Multiple Choice

1. To reveal the formatting codes, press

a. F6
b. Ctrl-F2
c. Alt-F3 (or F11)
d. F5
e. Shift-F7

2. The formatting code for centering text is

a. [CNTR] (text) [cntr]
b. [C] (text) [c]
c. [CENTER] (text) [center]
d. [CNTR] (text) [C/A/Flrt]
e. [CENTER] (text) [uncenter]

3. On the tab ruler, a tab stop is indicated by a

a. bracket
b. solid triangle
c. brace
d. parenthesis
e. star

4. To display the tab ruler, press Ctrl-F3 to display the menu. Select option 1 to get into the window. WordPerfect responds:

```
Number of lines in this window: 24
```

Next, you press

a. the down arrow
b. the left arrow
c. the right arrow
d. the up arrow
e. the Home key

5. A block of text can be

a. a character
b. a word
c. a series of words
d. an entire document
e. all of the above

6. To work with a block of data, move the cursor to the beginning of the data to be altered and press

a. Alt-F4 (or F12)
b. F8

  c. Shift-F5
  d. F3
  e. F7
7. Using the Block command and the Move command, WordPerfect can
  a. move text
  b. copy text
  c. delete text
  d. both a and c
  e. all of the above
8. During a search and replace operation, → tells you
  a. that WordPerfect will execute the command
  b. what you are searching for
  c. that WordPerfect will replace all occurrences automatically
  d. that WordPerfect will stop at each occurrence and await further instructions
  e. that WordPerfect will ignore all occurrences except the last
9. To enter a decimal tab, use the FORMAT function (Shift-F8) and, at the desired location on the ruler, select
  a. L
  b. R
  c. C
  d. D
  e. T
10. To make the date entry dynamic (so that it changes automatically), from the Shift-F5 (Date/Outline) menu select
  a. Date Code
  b. Date Text
  c. Date Format
  d. Outline
  e. Paragraph Number

True/False

1. There is no way to change the default margins and tab stops.
2. A decimal tab stop can be created that will align numbers on the decimal point.
3. You can enter the current system date (and time) automatically with the Shift-F5 (Date/Outline) command.
4. When using the search and replace option, there is a limit to the length of the word or words being replaced.
5. WordPerfect does not allow search and replace operations using lowercase characters.
6. While generating a document, WordPerfect adds special, invisible codes to the document.
7. The tab ruler displays only tab stops.
8. To display two documents at once, you begin with the Ctrl-F3 (Screen) command and shift between the two screens using Shift-F3 (Switch).
9. Cut and paste operations cannot be applied to tables.
10. Once you have deleted text, there is no way to undelete it.

ANSWERS

Multiple Choice

1. c
2. d
3. b
4. d
5. e
6. a
7. e
8. b
9. d
10. a

True/False

1. F
2. T
3. T
4. F
5. F
6. T
7. F
8. T
9. F
10. F

Layout Design and Merge Printing

6

6–1 INTRODUCTION

In this chapter we discuss various features of WordPerfect for designing the layout of your document. Creating page breaks, page numbers, headers, and footers are discussed. We also discuss the View Document command for reviewing a document before it is printed. The second part of this chapter reviews merge printing as one of the strongest features of WordPerfect. Merge printing enables you to combine fixed and variable documents, which is very helpful for mass mailings.

6–2 PAGE BREAKS

When you have entered enough text to fill one page, WordPerfect automatically enters a soft page break and moves to the next page. A soft page break is identified by a single-dashed line (-----). If you want to insert a page break manually, you must enter a hard page break.

To enter a hard page break, move the cursor to the desired position and press Ctrl-Enter. You will see a double-dashed line (=====). If you look at the status line, you see that the text typed after the double-dashed line is in page 2. Figure 6–1 shows a document with a hard page break. To remove a hard page break, move the cursor to the position of the break and press the Del key.

6–3 PAGE NUMBERS

You can number the pages of your document in several different ways. WordPerfect's default setting is without page numbers. Because page numbers do not show up on-screen, you must either print the document or use the View

```
     From: Tom Morris, Personnel
     To  : Administrative Staff

     Subject: WordPerfect Seminar

WordPerfect is one of the most popular word processing programs on
the market. The personnel office is planning to conduct a brief
seminar on this package.

================================================================================

Tom Morris from the personnel office will be the instructor. All
administrative staff are invited.

To encourage all of you to attend the seminar, there would be  cash
prizes awarded to three of the participants.

After familiarizing yourselves with WordPerfect, all of you who
participate will be given access to a PC with WordPerfect
capabilities.


A:\WORDPB\CH6-1.WP                                Doc 1 Pg 1 Ln 1" Pos 1"
```

Figure 6–1
A Document with a Hard Page Break

```
Format: Page

     1 - Center Page (top to bottom)    No

     2 - Force Odd/Even Page

     3 - Headers

     4 - Footers

     5 - Margins - Top                  1"
                   Bottom               1"

     6 - Page Numbering

     7 - Paper Size                     8.5" x 11"
               Type                     Standard

     8 - Suppress (this page only)



Selection: 0
```

Figure 6–2
Format: Page Menu

Document command to display the document on-screen. You can suppress the page-numbering feature whenever necessary. For example, you can number pages 1 through 6 and suppress the number on page 7. You can then resume the numbering from page 8 on.

Use the page-numbering feature to number the document presented in figure 6–1. To use the page-numbering feature, follow these steps:

1. Press Ctrl-Home. The prompt on the status line shows

```
Go to
```

2. Press 1 and Enter to move to the beginning of the document.
3. Press Shift-F8 to display the Format menu. Select option 2 for Page. You will see the Format: Page menu (see fig. 6–2). The prompt reads

```
Selection: 0
```

4. From this menu, select option 6. WordPerfect displays the Format: Page Numbering menu (see fig. 6–3).
5. From this menu, select option 4. You will see the menu shown in figure 6–4.
6. From this menu select option 2.
7. Press the spacebar three times to get back to your document.

If you print this document using Shift-F7 and 1 (Full Document), you will see that it is numbered and the page numbers appear at the top center of every page. This document is presented in figure 6–5. To suppress a page number, do the following:

1. Press Ctrl-Home. The status line reads

```
Go to
```

2. Type the number of the desired page.
3. Press Shift-F8 to display the Format menu. Select option 2.

Figure 6–3
Format: Page Numbering Menu

```
Format: Page Numbering

     1 - New Page Number       1

     2 - Page Number Style     ^B

     3 - Insert Page Number

     4 - Page Number Position No page numbering









Selection: 0
```

Figure 6–4
Page Number Position Menu

```
Format: Page Number Position

      Every Page                   Alternating Pages
     ┌───────────┐           ┌───────────┐ ┌───────────┐
     │ 1   2   3 │           │ 4         │ │         4 │
     │           │           │ Even      │ │       Odd │
     │ 5   6   7 │           │ 8         │ │         8 │
     └───────────┘           └───────────┘ └───────────┘

     9 - No Page Numbers






Selection: 0
```

```
                                  1

     From: Tom Morris, Personnel
     To  : Administrative Staff

     Subject: WordPerfect Seminar

WordPerfect is one of the most popular word processing programs on
the market. The personnel office is planning to conduct a brief
seminar on this package.
```

```
                                  2

Tom Morris from the personnel office will be the instructor. All
administrative staff are invited.

To encourage all of you to attend the seminar, there would be  cash
prizes awarded to three of the participants.

After familiarizing yourselves with WordPerfect, all of you who
participate will be given access to a PC with WordPerfect
capabilities.
```

Figure 6–5
A Document with Page Numbers

4. From the Page menu, select option 8 (Suppress). The Format: Suppress (This Page Only) menu is displayed.
5. From this menu, select option 4 (Suppress Page Numbering).
6. Press Y for Yes and Enter.
7. Press 0 twice to get back to your document. The page number for the desired page is suppressed.

From the Format: Page menu, you can select option 6 (New Page Number). You can enter any number up to 32,767. Your document will be numbered starting with this page number. Under option 1 of the Page Numbering menu, WordPerfect also gives you a choice of Arabic or Roman numerals.

6–4 PREVIEWING A DOCUMENT

When you add page numbers and other fancy features such as headers and footers to your document, you do not see these features until you print the document. By using the View Document command, you can see the layout of your document before it is printed. The View Document command, by generating a temporary document (Doc 3), displays headers, footers, footnotes, margins, and page numbers. You cannot perform any editing on this document, but you can view your document and return to the original to make corrections as needed.

Suppose that you want to preview the document presented in figure 6–5. Do the following:

1. Retrieve the document by pressing Shift-F10 and typing the file name.

2. Press Shift-F7 to display the Print menu. From this menu select option 6 (View Document). This option as default displays the entire page the cursor is on. Options 1 and 2 provide zoom features. Option 3 displays the full page. Option 4 displays facing pages.
3. You can see the page numbers that appear on the top center of each page.
4. Press F7 to return to your document.

6–5 INSERTING HEADERS AND FOOTERS INTO YOUR DOCUMENT

Headers are printed at the top of the page where the first line of text normally prints. **Footers** are printed on the last line. Suppose that you want to insert a header and a footer into the document presented in figure 6–5. To enter the header, do the following:

1. Move the cursor to the top of the page.
2. Press Shift-F8 and 2 to display the Format: Page menu.
3. From this menu, select option 3 for Headers or 4 for Footers. If you select option 3, WordPerfect displays the Headers menu (see fig. 6–6). As you can see, WordPerfect allows for two headers (A and B); it also allows for two footers. They can be on every page, on odd pages, or on even pages.
4. Select 1 for Header A. You will see the menu for header options (see fig. 6–7).
5. Select 2 from this menu for the header to appear on every page.
6. Next, type *Header-Testing* on the clear screen that WordPerfect provides.
7. Press F7 to exit and return to the Format: Page menu.
8. Press 0 twice to exit to the document.

Figure 6–6
The Headers Menu

```
Format: Page

     1 - Center Page (top to bottom)    No

     2 - Force Odd/Even Page

     3 - Headers

     4 - Footers

     5 - Margins - Top                  1"
                   Bottom               1"

     6 - Page Numbering

     7 - Paper Size                     8.5" x 11"
               Type                     Standard

     8 - Suppress (this page only)



1 Header A; 2 Header B: 0
```

```
Format: Page

     1 - Center Page (top to bottom)    No

     2 - Force Odd/Even Page

     3 - Headers

     4 - Footers

     5 - Margins - Top                  1"
                   Bottom               1"

     6 - Page Numbering

     7 - Paper Size                     8.5" x 11"
               Type                     Standard

     8 - Suppress (this page only)



1 Discontinue; 2 Every Page; 3 Odd Pages; 4 Even Pages; 5 Edit: 0
```

Figure 6–7
Header Options

Now you can preview your document and see that the header is inserted on the top of each page. Suppose that you want to insert a footer into your document. To do this, follow these steps:

1. Move the cursor to the beginning of the document.
2. Press Shift-F8 and 2 to display the Format: Page menu.
3. From this menu, select option 4 (Footers). You will see the Footers menu (see fig. 6–8).
4. Select 1 for Footer A.
5. Select 2 for Every Page. WordPerfect displays a blank screen.
6. Type *Footer-Testing* and press F7 to exit to the Format: Page menu.
7. Press 0 twice to exit to the document.

To print this document, press Shift-F7. Make sure that your printer is on-line, and then select option 1 (Full Document). Your report should look like the one in figure 6–9. If you preview this document, you will see that the header is at the top and the footer is at the bottom in both pages.

6–6 CHANGING HEADERS AND FOOTERS

You can change headers and footers after they are inserted, and you can make them underlined or bold. To display and change the header in figure 6–9, follow these steps:

1. Press Shift-F8 and select 2 to display the Format: Page menu.
2. From this menu, select option 3 (Headers).

Figure 6–8
The Footers Menu

```
Format: Page

     1 - Center Page (top to bottom)    No

     2 - Force Odd/Even Page

     3 - Headers

     4 - Footers

     5 - Margins - Top                  1"
                   Bottom               1"

     6 - Page Numbering

     7 - Paper Size                     8.5" x 11"
               Type                     Standard

     8 - Suppress (this page only)



1 Footer A; 2 Footer B: 0
```

```
Header-Testing                  1


     From: Tom Morris, Personnel
     To  : Administrative Staff

     Subject: WordPerfect Seminar

WordPerfect is one of the most popular word processing programs on
the market. The personnel office is planning to conduct a brief
seminar on this package.

Footer-Testing
```

```
Header-Testing                  2


Tom Morris from the personnel office will be the instructor. All
administrative staff are invited.

To encourage all of you to attend the seminar, there would be  cash
prizes awarded to three of the participants.

After familiarizing yourselves with WordPerfect, all of you who
participate  will  be  given  access  to  a  PC  with  WordPerfect
capabilities.

Footer-Testing
```

Figure 6–9
A Report with Page Numbers, a Header, and a Footer

3. Select option 1 (Header A).
4. Choose option 5 for Edit. WordPerfect displays the "Header-Testing" header that you inserted. You can make any changes to it by using the editing features of WordPerfect.
5. When you are finished, press F7 to exit to the Format: Page menu.
6. Press 0 twice to return to your document.

6–7 MERGE PRINTING

There are many times when an organization sends the same letter to several hundred or thousand of its customers. Typing individual letters to all the customers would be an impossibly time-consuming task. WordPerfect provides a **merge printing** feature that can expedite this process. Merge printing can be particularly helpful for form letters, for standard billing documents, for promotional letters, for brochures describing new products, and for organizational notices.

In merge printing, you have a **constant document** (sometimes called a "boiler plate") and a **variable document** that contains the variable information. The constant document might be an organizational notice, and the variable document might be the mailing list, for example.

The variable data are entered into the constant file from the keyboard or from a computer file stored on a secondary storage device, such as a floppy or a hard disk. Codes in the constant document can indicate where information from the variable document should be inserted. If data are being entered from the secondary file, the codes refer to the fields in that file. One code represents one field of data—first name or last name, for example. It is up to you to define the amount of information to be considered as a field. It depends on how you set up your variable document.

6–8 MERGE CODES

WordPerfect uses a series of codes for merge printing. Table 6–1 summarizes these **merge codes,** which are found under More in the Shift-F9 (Merge Codes) menu. Figure 6–10 shows the Merge Codes menu. To display the Merge Codes menu press Shift-F9 and select More.

6–9 CREATING A CONSTANT DOCUMENT

To create the constant document (the form letter) start WordPerfect. To create the document presented in figure 6–11 complete the following steps:

1. Press Shift-F9 to display the Merge Codes menu.
2. From this menu select 6 (More). WordPerfect will open a window on the right. Highlight the date code and press Enter to enter the system date in the letter and then press Enter again.
3. Press Shift-F9 to display the Merge Codes menu.
4. Highlight {FIELD}, and then press Enter. WordPerfect responds:

```
Enter Field:
```

Type 1, press Enter two times, and press Shift-F9.

Table 6–1
Merge Codes

{Keyboard} ^C	Temporarily stops the merge, allowing text to be entered from the keyboard. Press the F9 key to continue. If a ^C is found in the constant or variable file, the merge will pause so that you may type in text. When you press F9 the merging will continue.
{Date} ^D	Inserts the system date (which should be entered as the current date when the system is booted).
{End Record} ^E	Marks the end of a record in a secondary file. Press the Merge E key to stop a merge.
{Field} ^Fn^	Merges the text from field n (where n = 1, 2, 3, and so on) into the document being created.
{Chain Macro} ^G	The command ^Gmacro name^G starts the named macro at the end of the merge.
{Next Record} ^N	Looks for the next record in the secondary file. If it does not find the next record it ends the merge process.
{Prompt} Message	The command ^Omessage^O displays the message on the status line and is generally used with the ^C code.
{Quit} ^Q	Stops the merge process.
{End Field} ^R	Marks the end of a field in a secondary file. (Generate this code by pressing F9.)
{Subst Secondary} ^S	The command ^Sfilename^S will change to the named secondary file.
{Print} ^T	Sends all text that has been merged to the point of {Print} to the printer.
{Rewrite} ^U	Updates (rewrites) the screen.
{Mrg Cmnd} ^V	Lets you transfer merge codes into the document being created.

```
1 Field; 2 End Record; 3 Input; 4 Page Off; 5 Next Record; 6 More: 0
```

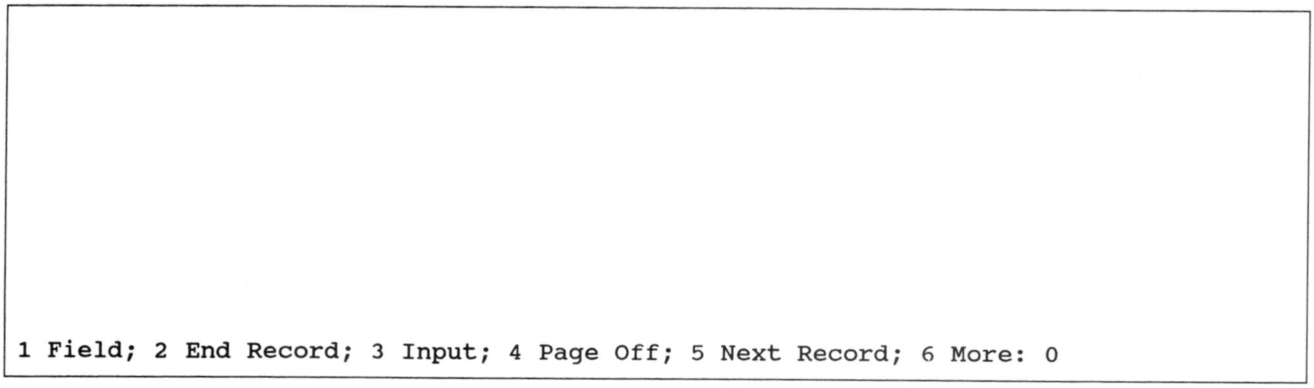

Figure 6–10
The Merge Codes Menu

```
{DATE}

{FIELD}1~
{FIELD}2~
{FIELD}3~


Dear {FIELD}4~:

     I am pleased to inform you that the credit department has
approved your credit request.

Sincerely yours,




Mary Fishler
Credit Manager




A:\WORDP\CH6-11.WPP                        Doc 1 Pg 1 Ln 4.33" Pos 1"
```

Figure 6–11
A Sample Form Letter

5. Highlight {FIELD} and press Enter. WordPerfect responds:

```
Enter Field:
```

Type 2 and press Enter two times

6. Press Shift-F9. Highlight {FIELD} and press Enter. WordPerfect responds

```
Enter Field:
```

Type 3 and press Enter five times.

7. Type *Dear* and press the spacebar.
8. Press Shift-F9. Highlight {FIELD} and press Enter. WordPerfect responds:

```
Enter Field:
```

Type 4 and press Enter.

9. Enter a colon (:) and press Enter twice.
10. Press the Tab key, and then type the following:

    I am pleased to inform you that the credit department has approved your credit request.

11. Press Enter twice, type *Sincerely yours,* and press Enter four times.
12. Type *Mary Fishler* and press Enter. Type *Credit Manager* and press Enter.

Save this document by pressing F10 and name it CH6-11.WP.

6–10

CREATING A VARIABLE DOCUMENT

To create the mailing list file (the variable document), do the following:

1. On a clear screen, type *Mr. John Jones*. From the More menu, enter an {End Field} code (this marks the end of the field).
2. Type *3100 Ashe Road, #200* and then from the More menu, enter an {End Field} code.
3. Type *Portland, OR 97201* and from the More menu, enter an {End Field} code.
4. Type *Mr. Jones*. From the More menu enter an {End Field} code.
5. Press Shift-F9 and enter an {End Record} code.

This marks the end of the first record. It also places a hard page break after each record. Now you must enter the second record as follows:

1. Type *Ms. Dona Brown* and from the More menu, enter an {End Field} code to mark the end of the first field.
2. Type *1627 Broadway Avenue, #11* and enter an {End Field} code.
3. Type *San Diego, CA 92112* and enter an {End Field} code.
4. Type *Ms. Brown* and enter an {End Field} code.
5. From the More menu enter another {End Record} code.

This marks the end of the second record. It also creates a hard page break. This file is displayed in figure 6–12. Save your file using the F10 key and name it CH6-12.WP.

```
Mr. John Jones{END FIELD}
3100 Ashe Rd #200{END FIELD}
Portland, OR 97201{END FIELD}
Mr. Jones{END FIELD}
{END RECORD}
================================================================================
Ms. Dona Brown{END FIELD}
1627 Broadway Ave #11{END FIELD}
San Diego, CA 92112{END FIELD}
Ms. Brown{END FIELD}
{END RECORD}
================================================================================









Field: 1                                             Doc 1 Pg 1 Ln 1" Pos 1"
```

Figure 6–12
A Variable File

6–11 STARTING THE MERGE PRINT OPERATION

To merge the constant file (see fig. 6–11) and the variable file (see fig. 6–12), do the following:

1. On a clear screen, press Ctrl-F9. The following menu will be displayed:

```
1 Merge; 2 Sort; 3 Convert Old Merge Codes: 0
```

2. From this menu, select option 1 (Merge). The status line displays:

```
Primary file:
```

3. Enter *A:CH6-11.WP,* which is the name of your primary file. Press Enter. The status line now displays:

```
Secondary file:
```

4. Enter *A:CH6-12.WP* (the name of the secondary file) and press Enter. WordPerfect responds

```
*Merging*
```

and both letters are displayed on-screen. However, you will see only the second letter—the first letter has been scrolled up. You can use the PgUp key to see the first one. The current date is inserted on the top of both letters. These sample letters are shown in figures 6–13 and 6–14.

When you establish your variable file, you should remember that all the records must be consistent. For example, if one of the fields is missing, you must still enter it as {End Field}. Suppose that in a mailing list you include four fields

```
January 1, 1991


Mr. John Jones
3100 Ashe Rd #200
Portland, OR 97201


Dear Mr. Jones:

     I am pleased to inform you that the credit department has
approved your credit request.

Sincerely yours,




Mary Fishler
Credit Manager
```

Figure 6–13
The First Sample Letter

```
January 1, 1991

Ms. Dona Brown
1627 Broadway Ave #11
San Diego, CA 92112


Dear Ms. Brown:

     I am pleased to inform you that the credit department has
approved your credit request.

Sincerely yours,



Mary Fishler
Credit Manager
```

Figure 6–14
The Second Sample Letter

for each customer—NAME, TITLE, ADDRESS, and CITY/STATE. If one of your customers doesn't have a title, for that customer you must enter {End Field} for field 2 to indicate that this field exists, but it is empty for this particular customer.

In the top part of the letter, if you want to address the customer by first name, just type the first name. In the example, field 4 would be John {End Field} or Dona {End Field}. If you want to have both first and last names appear, enter field 4 as Mr. John Jones {End Field} or Ms. Dona Brown {End Field}.

6–12 MAKING MERGE PRINTING AN INTERACTIVE PROCESS

You can insert codes in the constant file to make merge printing an interactive process. For example, if in your constant document you have a word or phrase that will vary depending on which customer you are referring to, **interactive merge printing** enables you to insert the desired information while merge printing is taking place.

Using your constant and variable documents from the example, suppose that you want to inform each customer of the line of credit for which they have been approved. Do the following:

1. Retrieve the constant document file, A:CH6-11.WP, and move the cursor to the information you want to alter. In this case, you want your letter to read:

   I am pleased to inform you that the credit department has approved your credit request of

2. After typing *request of,* display the Merge Codes menu, and from the More menu, choose Input. WordPerfect responds

```
Enter Message:
```

3. Type *enter amount* and press Enter.

```
{DATE}

{FIELD}1~
{FIELD}2~
{FIELD}3~


Dear {FIELD}4~:

     I am pleased to inform you that the credit department has
approved your credit request of {INPUT}Enter Amount~.

Sincerely yours,



Mary Fishler
Credit Manager
{PAGE OFF}{PRINT}


A:\WORDP\CH6-15.WP                              Doc 1 Pg 1 Ln 4.33" Pos 1"
```

Figure 6–15
A Constant Document with Keyboard Input and Codes for Printing

This Input code will stop the execution of the merge printing process and wait for your input. The prompt appears only on-screen, not on the printer. When you are finished, the last line of your letter should read:

your credit request of {input} enter amount ~.

To complete the interactive process, you must press F9 after inserting the variable text. To tell the computer to send the merged text to the printer, you must end your constant file with the merge print codes {Print} and {Page Off}. {Print} sends the merged text to the printer; {Page Off} tells the program to go to the next record in the secondary file and to use the same constant file each time. Figure 6–15 illustrates this example.

6–13 PULL-DOWN MENU HIGHLIGHTS

1. To make a page break, select Layout from the main menu. Then select Align and Hard Page.
2. To do page numbering, choose Layout from the main menu, and then select Page and option 6.
3. To preview a document, select File from the main menu. Then select Print and option 6.
4. To insert headers or footers into your document, choose Layout from the main menu. From the Layout menu select Page, and then select Headers or Footers (option 3 or 4).
5. To display merge codes, choose Tools from the main menu, and then pick Merge Codes. From the Merge Codes menu, you can select the desired merge code option.

6. To start the merge operation, from the main menu, choose Tools, and then Merge. Identify the primary file and press Enter; then specify the secondary file and press Enter.

SUMMARY

In this chapter we reviewed various aspects of WordPerfect for designing the layout of a document, including page breaks, page numbers, headers, and footers. We discussed the View Document command for reviewing a document before it is printed. The second part of the chapter reviewed merge printing for combining a fixed and a variable document.

REVIEW QUESTIONS

*These questions are answered in Appendix A.

1. What is a soft page break?
2. What is a hard page break?
3. How is a soft page break entered? Is this the user's responsibility or WordPerfect's responsibility?
*4. How do you enter a hard page break? How do you remove a hard page break?
5. How do you display the Page Number menu?
*6. Can page numbers be placed anywhere on the document or are they always in a fixed position?
7. How do you preview a document? What is displayed when you preview a document?
*8. Can you edit a document in the Preview mode?
9. How do you enter a header in your document?
10. How do you enter a footer in your document?
11. Can you change a header or a footer after it is inserted? If yes, how do you do this?
12. What is merge printing?
13. What are the applications of merge printing?
*14. What are merge codes? What do they do?
15. What code is used to mark the end of a field? The end of a record?
16. How do you create a fixed document? A variable document?
*17. How do you get the merge process started?
18. How do you know the merge process has been a success?
19. Can you make merge printing an interactive process? If so, how?
20. How do you send the result of merge printing to the printer?

HANDS-ON EXPERIENCE

1. Type figure 6–1 into your computer and do the following:
   a. Insert a hard page break after every paragraph.
   b. Number the four pages of the document from 1 to 4. The page number should be at the bottom center of every page.
   c. Preview this document to see if the page numbers are entered properly.
   d. Suppress the page number on page 2 of the document. Use the View Document command to verify your work.
   e. Insert a header on every even numbered page.
   f. Delete this header and enter a header on all the odd numbered pages.
   g. Insert a footer on all the even numbered pages. Using the View Document command, verify your work.

h. Change the header to "New Header."

i. Change the footer to "New Footer."

2. Use the merge printing feature of WordPerfect to merge the following two documents. The constant document is

> Dear Valued Customer:
>
> I am pleased to announce that we are opening a new branch of our department store in your neighborhood. There is a grand opening party on the first Tuesday of next month. You and your family are invited to attend. We are looking forward to seeing you there.
>
> Sincerely,
>
> John Thomson
> Marketing Manager

The variable document is

> Ms. Susan Smith
> Chief Executive Officer
> 16201 South Jefferson
> Portland, OR 97201
>
> Mr. Tony Adam
> 151 North Cliff
> San Diego, CA 92112
>
> Ms. Mary Thomas
> Product Manager
> 1691 East Hampton
> Denver, CO 80209

3. Retrieve the exercise document from your disk and do the following:
   a. Number each page of this document at center bottom using Roman numerals (i, ii, iii).
   b. Set a top margin of 4 inches and a bottom margin of 2 inches. Print the document. How does it look?
   c. Use the View Document command to preview this document.
   d. Try all four options of the View Document command. What are the applications of the zoom feature?
   e. Insert the following header and footer into your document:

      Header—This is a practice document
      Footer—This document will be saved under New

   f. Save this document under New.
4. Try all the merge codes presented in Table 6–1. What are specific applications of each?

KEY TERMS

Constant document
Footers
Headers
Interactive merge printing
Merge codes
Merge printing
Variable document

KEY COMMANDS

Display the Format: Page menu (Shift-F8)

Display the Merge Codes menu (Shift-F9)

Display the Merge menu (Ctrl-F9)

Enter a hard page break (Ctrl-Enter)

Turn the page number feature on (Ctrl-Home)

Delete a character or a hard page break (Del)

Enter an ^R code to mark the end of a field (Shift-F9)

Display the Print menu (Shift-F7)

Enter an ^E code to mark the end of a record (Shift-F9)

Retrieve a document from a disk (Shift-F10)

MISCONCEPTIONS AND SOLUTIONS

Misconception Merge printing does not generate information in the order you want.

Solution Sort the secondary (variable document) file based on any desired key, and then start the merge operations. (The sort operation is discussed in the next chapter.)

Misconception When you start the merge printing operation, you may not want to see the entire process, and you must stop the merge operation.

Solution Press Shift-F9 to stop merge printing.

Misconception Sometimes you would like to generate a partial merge print from the secondary document. To generate the whole list and use half of it would be a waste of resources.

Solution You can enter a ^Q code into your secondary document at the point you want to stop merge printing.

DIFFERENCES BETWEEN WORDPERFECT 4.2 AND 5.0

- In WordPerfect 4.2, to display the Format menu, you must press Shift-F8. The screen displayed in WordPerfect 4.2 is different than in WordPerfect 5.0. However, the contents are nearly the same.
- In WordPerfect 4.2, headers and footers are in the same menu.
- The Page menu is slightly different in WordPerfect 4.2.
- In WordPerfect 4.2, to display the Merge Codes menu, you must press Shift-F9.
- In WordPerfect 4.2, the ^E code does not place a hard page break after each record.
- In WordPerfect 4.2, when you press Ctrl-F9, the following menu is displayed:

```
1 Merge; 2 Sort; 3 Sorting Sequences: 0
```

DIFFERENCES BETWEEN WORDPERFECT 5.0 AND 5.1

- In WordPerfect 5.0, the merge codes are very different. The new merge codes in WordPerfect 5.1 are easier to use.
- In WordPerfect 5.1, the merge codes are actual words, allowing easy recognition of each code's purpose.
- In WordPerfect 5.0, when you press Ctrl-F9 you see:

```
1 Merge; 2 Sort:0
```

- In WordPerfect 5.0, the Page Numbering menu is different. It is now much easier to place page numbers inside a document, and it is also easy to include text with the page number.

ARE YOU READY TO MOVE ON?

Multiple Choice

1. A soft page break is identified by
   - **a.** a single-dashed line (---)
   - **b.** a double-dashed line (===)
   - **c.** a line of asterisks (***)
   - **d.** a line of plus signs (+++)
   - **e.** none of the above
2. To enter a hard page break, place the cursor in the desired position and press
   - **a.** Enter
   - **b.** the Backspace key
   - **c.** Ctrl-Enter
   - **d.** Ctrl-Backspace
   - **e.** Ctrl-Home
3. Page numbering is available from the
   - **a.** Format: Line menu
   - **b.** Format: Page menu
   - **c.** Format: Document menu
   - **d.** Format: Other menu
   - **e.** Format: Disk menu
4. To preview a document, use the View Document option available by pressing
   - **a.** Ctrl-F5 (Text In/Out)
   - **b.** Shift-F8 (Format)
   - **c.** Alt-F9 (Graphics)
   - **d.** Shift-F7 (Print)
   - **e.** none of the above
5. The View Document preview feature can
   - **a.** display a single page of the document at a time
   - **b.** zoom in 100 percent
   - **c.** zoom in 200 percent
   - **d.** display facing pages
   - **e.** all of the above
6. The Header or Footer menu is selected from the
   - **a.** Format: Line menu
   - **b.** Format: Page menu
   - **c.** Format: Document menu
   - **d.** Format: Other menu
   - **e.** Format: Disk menu
7. In merge printing, WordPerfect makes use of two documents—a constant document and a non-constant document—which are sometimes referred to as
   - **a.** boiler-plate and variable documents
   - **b.** bold and underlined documents

   c. letter and address documents
   d. variable and secondary documents
   e. none of the above

8. To create a constant document (for example, a form letter), the merge code to insert at each variable field is
   a. ^E
   b. ^C
   c. ^O
   d. ^F
   e. ^R

9. To create a variable document (for example, a mailing list), the merge code to insert to mark the end of each field is
   a. ^E
   b. ^C
   c. ^O
   d. ^F
   e. ^R

10. When ^E is placed in the variable document, it signifies
   a. the end of a field
   b. the end of a line
   c. the end of a record
   d. the end of a page
   e. none of the above

True/False

1. As soon as you enter enough text to fill a page, WordPerfect automatically enters a soft page break and moves to the next page.

2. There is no method available to remove a hard page break, so you must be positive that you want to place one in your document.

3. If you decide to include page numbers in your document, they will not display on the standard edit screen; you must either print the document or use the View Document feature.

4. Once page numbering is turned on, a page number must be placed on every page.

5. While previewing a document using the View Document feature, you can edit and make any changes desired.

6. You can define as many as two headers and two footers in a document.

7. Once they are created, headers and footers cannot be changed.

8. WordPerfect has no provision for merge printing.

9. A variable data item in the constant document is denoted by a special merge code that links that item to a specific field in the variable document.

10. The ^C code is used to momentarily pause the merge operation and ask for input from the console (keyboard).

ANSWERS

Multiple Choice

1. a
2. c
3. b
4. d
5. e
6. b
7. a
8. d
9. e
10. c

True/False

1. T
2. F
3. T
4. F
5. F
6. T
7. F
8. F
9. T
10. T

Using WordPerfect Advanced Features: Part I

7

7–1 INTRODUCTION

In this chapter we introduce four advanced features of WordPerfect: footnotes and endnotes, subscripts and superscripts, sort operations, and line drawing. The first two features assist you in writing scientific- and research-oriented documents. Sort operations help you to perform limited data-management operations on your document. Line-drawing features enable you to draw boxes and charts in your document.

7–2 ENTERING FOOTNOTES

When you write a term paper or conduct a research project, you must provide citations to the published materials. **Footnotes** are citations printed at the bottom of the page on which the references were made. If you want to put all your citations at the end of a chapter or section, you are creating **endnotes.** Besides the location of printing, there are no other differences between footnotes and endnotes.

When you cite a published work, you enter a footnote or endnote number after the author's name at the point in your document where the work is referenced. WordPerfect automatically numbers the citations for you. If later you delete one or several of the citations, WordPerfect automatically renumbers the remaining footnotes and references. It is very easy to insert or delete footnotes between existing notes.

There are three common formats for entering footnotes: APA (American Psychological Association), MLA (Modern Language Association), and Turabian format. You can choose any one of these styles and enter the citation as indicated.

Suppose that you want to enter the following paragraph and make two citations:

> Decision Support Systems (DSS) are designed to assist decision makers in all levels of the organization. Lotus 1-2-3, which has gained popularity in recent years, is used as a DSS tool.

The first citation should be entered right after the word "organization." The second citation should be entered after the word "tool." The two citations are as follows:

[1]Bidgoli, Hossein. Decision Support Systems: Principles & Practice. St. Paul: West Publishing Company, 1989.

[2]Bidgoli, Hossein. Working with Lotus 1-2-3: A Comprehensive Manual. St. Paul: West Publishing Company, 1991.

To enter these citations, follow these steps:

1. Move the cursor to the space after the word "organization."
2. Press Ctrl-F7 to display the Note menu. From this menu select 1 for Footnote.
3. From the Footnote menu, select option 1 (Create). You see a screen with number 1 on the top of the screen.
4. Type the first citation. Remember to underline the title of the book by using the F8 (Underline) key.
5. Press F7 to exit.

```
     Decision Support Systems (DSS) are designed to assist decision
makers in all levels of the organization(1). Lotus 1-2-3 has gained
a lot of popularity in recent years; it is used as a DSS tool(2).




____________________

     1Bidgoli, Hossein. Decision Support Systems: Principles &
Practice. St. Paul: West Publishing Company, 1989.

     2Bidgoli, Hossein. Working With Lotus 1-2-3: A Comprehensive
Manual. St. Paul: West Publishing Company, 1991.
```

Figure 7–1
A Document with Two Footnotes

To enter the second citation, follow these steps:

1. Move the cursor to the space after the word "tool."
2. Press Ctrl-F7 to display the Note menu. Select 1 for Footnote.
3. From the Footnote menu, choose option 1 (Create). Number 2 is displayed at the top of the screen.
4. Enter the second citation. Underline the title of the book by using the F8 (Underline) key.
5. Press F7 to exit.

If you preview this document, you will see both footnotes. This document is illustrated in figure 7–1.

7–3 EDITING EXISTING FOOTNOTES

You may make mistakes when entering citations, but you easily can correct them using the editing feature of WordPerfect. To edit a footnote, do the following:

1. Move the cursor to the beginning of the document.
2. Press Ctrl-F7 to display the Note menu. Select 1 for Footnote.
3. From the Footnote menu, select option 2 (Edit). WordPerfect responds:

```
Footnote Number?1
```

This means that you can edit footnote 1. If you want to edit any other footnote, just enter the number. If you press Enter, footnote 1 is displayed for editing.

4. Press F7 to return to the document.

7–4 CHANGING FOOTNOTE OPTIONS

When you create footnotes or endnotes, they are entered using WordPerfect's default setting. However, WordPerfect provides a variety of options from which you can choose. To choose from these options, do the following:

1. Press Ctrl-F7 to display the Note menu. Select 1 for Footnote.
2. Select option 4 from this menu. WordPerfect displays the menu shown in figure 7–2. You can choose any of these options by moving the cursor to the particular option and selecting it.
3. Press 0 to return to your document.

7–5 SUPERSCRIPT AND SUBSCRIPT

In scientific reports, there are times when you have to use **superscript** (text above the line) or **subscript** (text below the line). Different word processing programs and printers handle these features differently. WordPerfect allows both features. In figure 7–3, you can see the following equations:

X1 + X2 = 10
X1 − X2 = 5

```
Footnote Options

     1 - Spacing Within Footnotes          1
                 Between Footnotes         0.167"

     2 - Amount of Note to Keep Together   0.5"

     3 - Style for Number in Text          [SUPRSCPT][Note Num][suprscpt]

     4 - Style for Number in Note               [SUPRSCPT][Note Num][suprscpt

     5 - Footnote Numbering Method         Numbers

     6 - Start Footnote Numbers each Page  No

     7 - Line Separating Text and Footnotes 2-inch Line

     8 - Print Continued Message           No

     9 - Footnotes at Bottom of Page       Yes


Selection: 0
```

Figure 7–2
Footnote Options

```
          An Example Of Linear Equation (Subscripts Example)

               X1 + X2  = 10
               X1 - X2  = 5



          An Example Of Exponentiation (Superscripts Example)

            1 Byte = 23   Bits
            1 K    = 210  Bytes




1 Size; 2 Appearance; 3 Normal; 4 Base Font; 5 Print Color: 0
```

Figure 7–3
A Sample Document Using Subscript and Superscript

Suppose that you want the numbers 1 and 2 to be printed as subscripts. Also in figure 7–3 is the following text:

1 Byte = 23 Bits
1 K = 210 Bytes

You want to print the 3 in 23 and the 10 in 210 as superscripts. Do the following:

1. Move the cursor to the 1 of X1.
2. Press Alt-F4 or F12 to turn on the Block feature.
3. Use the right-arrow key to highlight the 1.
4. Press Ctrl-F8 to display the Superscript/Subscript menu.
5. From this menu, select 1 for Size. You will see the menu shown in figure 7–4.
6. Choose 2 (Subscript).

Follow these same steps for the rest of the variables. To print superscript, do the following:

1. Move the cursor to the 3 of 23.
2. Press Alt-F4 or F12 to turn on the Block feature.
3. Using the right-arrow key, highlight the 3.
4. Press Ctrl-F8 and then the 1 (Size).
5. From the Size menu, select 1 for Superscript.

```
An Example Of Linear Equation (Subscripts Example)

     X1 + X2  = 10
     X1 - X2  = 5



An Example Of Exponentiation (Superscripts Example)

  1 Byte = 23   Bits
  1 K    = 210  Bytes




1 Suprscpt; 2 Subscpt; 3 Fine; 4 Small; 5 Large; 6 Vry Large; 7 Ext Large: 0
```

Figure 7–4
The Size Menu

The superscripted text will be highlighted. Repeat these steps to make the 10 of 210 a superscript. Use Shift-F7 to print the document (see fig. 7–5). As you can see, the superscripts and subscripts are part of the document.

The procedure just described is used if the text has already been typed in. You can also enter text as superscript or subscript. For example, suppose that you want to enter X12 with the 12 as a subscript. Type *X* and then press Ctrl-F8. From the menu, select 1 (Size). Next, select 2 (Subscript). Type *12*. The 12 will be highlighted in a box. To terminate the process, press Ctrl-F8 and, from the menu, choose 3 (Normal).

An Example Of Linear Equation (Subscripts Example)

$X_1 + X_2 = 10$
$X_1 - X_2 = 5$

An Example Of Exponentiation (Superscripts Example)

1 Byte = 2^3 Bits
1 K = 2^{10} Bytes

Figure 7–5
An Example of Subscript and Superscript

7-6 SORT OPERATIONS

WordPerfect offers some limited data-management operations, including **sort operations.** To perform sort operations you first must decide how much of the document is going to be sorted. It can be the entire document, several paragraphs, one paragraph, a block, or a column. You also must decide which key you want for the sort. The key is the information used by WordPerfect for sorting your document. For example, an account number, last name, credit limit, and so forth.

To create a comprehensive sorted file the sort key should be unique, such as a social security or account number. If the **primary key** is not unique, you must use a **secondary key** to sort when duplicate primary keys occur. For example, if your document includes 10 customers with the last name Brown, you must use a secondary key to distinguish among the Browns. WordPerfect allows up to nine sort keys. Finally, you must decide how you want the data sorted--in **ascending order** or **descending order.**

WordPerfect uses the following sorting sequence:

1. Special characters, such as @ and #
2. Numbers 0 through 9
3. Uppercase letters
4. Lowercase letters

To show you how sort operations work, let us walk through some examples. Suppose that you want to create the following table, which is a part of the customer database of Alpha-Talk, a manufacturer of wooden products:

FNAME	LNAME	SEX	AGE	CREDIT
Bob	Brown	M	33	1000
Jan	Brown	F	80	2000
Tom	Brown	M	21	9000
Mary	Smith	F	31	1200
Marty	Thomson	M	52	2500
Sandy	Jones	F	26	1100
Brian	Vigen	M	51	5000

To create this document, you must set up tabs. Follow these steps:

1. Press Shift-F8 to display the Format menu. Choose option 1 (Line).
2. From this menu, select option 8 (Tab Set).
3. Press Home and the left-arrow key to move to position 0", and then press Ctrl-End to delete all tab stops. The tab ruler is represented by a series of dots.
4. Select T and A to select absolute tab stops.
5. Press 1 and Enter. Type *2.2* and press Enter. Type *3.4* and press Enter. Type *4.6* and press Enter. Finally, type *5.8* and press Enter to set tabs at positions 1", 2.2", 3.4", 4.6", and 5.8".
6. Press F7 to exit to the menu. Press Enter twice to return to a clear screen.
7. Type *FNAME* (this is in position 1").
8. Press Tab and type *LNAME*.

```
FNAME      LNAME      SEX      AGE      CREDIT
Bob        Brown      M        33       1000
Jan        Brown      F        80       2000
Tom        Brown      M        21       9000
Mary       Smith      F        31       1200
Marty      Thomson    M        52       2500
Sandy      Jones      F        26       1100
Brian      Vigen      M        51       5000

A:\WORDPB\CH7-6.WP                        Doc 1 Pg 1 Ln 1" Pos 1"
```

Figure 7–6
A Sample Table for Sort Operations

9. Press Tab and type *SEX*.
10. Press Tab and type *AGE*.
11. Press Tab, type *CREDIT,* and press Enter.
12. Enter the data for the table until the entire table is constructed (see fig. 7–6).

7–7 SORTING BY LINES

Suppose that you want to sort the table shown in figure 7–6 by lines. The sort block of data will extend from Bob Brown to Brian Vigen. You should not include the headings in your block. If you do, they will be sorted with your data. In this table, the first tab is in the margin position (position 1″). To sort this table by lines, follow these steps:

1. Move the cursor to the first "B" of Bob Brown.
2. Press Alt-F4 to turn on the Block feature.
3. Highlight the entire block by moving the cursor to the right (to 1000), and then down to Brian Vigen.
4. Press Ctrl-F9 to display the Sort By Line menu (see fig. 7–7).

This menu shows the default settings. The default setting for the primary key is the first field and, for the sort order, the default is ascending. The default type for the first field is alphanumeric. These settings fit your table description and the sort you want to perform. Select 1 for Perform Action. WordPerfect will sort your table by the first field in ascending order. The sorted table is shown in figure 7–8.

```
FNAME       LNAME       SEX         AGE         CREDIT
Bob         Brown       M           33          1000
Jan         Brown       F           80          2000
Tom         Brown       M           21          9000
Mary        Smith       F           31          1200
Marty       Thomson     M           52          2500
Sandy       Jones       F           26          1100
Brian       Vigen       M           51          5000

                                                   Doc 2 Pg 1 Ln 1" POS 1"
{   ▲    ▲    ▲    ▲    ▲    ▲    ▲    ▲    ▲    ▲    ▲    ▲    }    ▲    ▲
--------------------------------- Sort by Line ---------------------------------

Key Typ Field Word          Key Typ Field Word          Key Typ Field Word
 1   a    1     1            2                           3
 4                           5                           6
 7                           8                           9
Select

Action                      Order                       Type
Sort                        Ascending                   Line sort

1 Perform Action; 2 View; 3 Keys; 4 Select; 5 Action; 6 Order; 7 Type: 0
```

Figure 7–7
Sort By Line Menu

```
FNAME       LNAME       SEX         AGE         CREDIT
Bob         Brown       M           33          1000
Brian       Vigen       M           51          5000
Jan         Brown       F           80          2000
Marty       Thomson     M           52          2500
Mary        Smith       F           31          1200
Sandy       Jones       F           26          1100
Tom         Brown       M           21          9000

A:\WORDPB\CH7-8.WP                               Doc 1 Pg 1 Ln 1.17" Pos 1"
```

Figure 7–8
Sort By One Key

```
FNAME      LNAME      SEX    AGE    CREDIT
Sandy      Jones      F      26     1100
Mary       Smith      F      31     1200
Jan        Brown      F      80     2000
Tom        Brown      M      21     9000
Bob        Brown      M      33     1000
Brian      Vigen      M      51     5000
Marty      Thomson    M      52     2500

A:\WORDPB\CH7-9.WP                    Doc 1 Pg 1 Ln 1" Pos 1"
```

Figure 7–9
Table Sorted by SEX and AGE

7–8 SORTING BY TWO KEYS

Suppose that you want to sort the table in figure 7–6 by sex and age. SEX is the primary key and AGE is the secondary key. When the sort is finished, you should see all the female customers followed by all the male customers. The customers will be listed in ascending order by their age. To do this, follow these steps:

1. Move the cursor to the "B" of Bob and press Alt-F4 or F12 to turn on the Block feature.
2. Highlight all the data except the headings.
3. Press Ctrl-F9 to display the Sort By Line menu.
4. Select option 3 (Keys). Make Key 1 field 3 (SEX). To do this, move the cursor to Field and choose 3. The type is "a" for alphanumeric. Make Key 2 field 4 (AGE) and specify Numeric (n) as the type.
5. Press F7 and choose 1 (Perform Action). The result is shown in figure 7–9.

7–9 LINE DRAWING

Sometimes you may want to highlight a portion of text by placing it in a box, or you may want to draw simple charts, such as organization charts, structure charts, or command maps. WordPerfect's **line drawing** feature enables you to perform all these tasks. Be aware, however, that you may not be able to print the charts and graphs generated by WordPerfect on your printer. You may have to acquire certain fonts. Consult your printer manual.

To display the Screen menu, press Ctrl-F3. Next, select option 2 (Line Draw). Figure 7–10 shows the Line Draw menu.

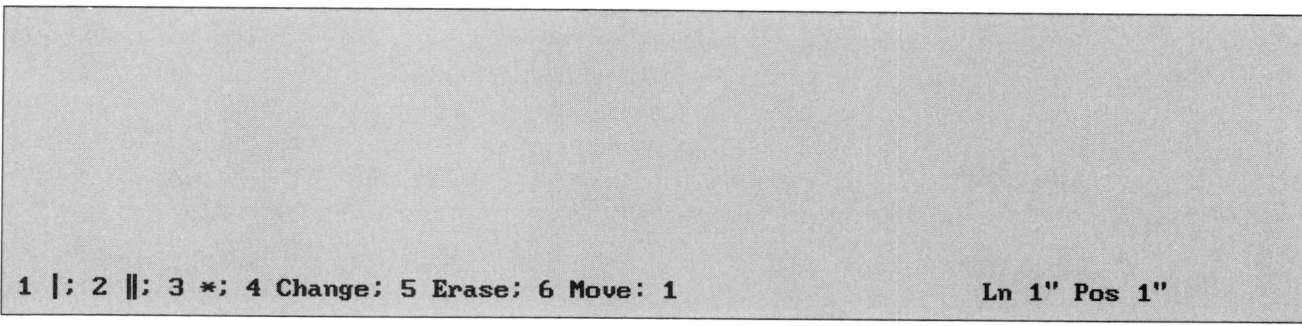

Figure 7–10
The Line Draw Menu

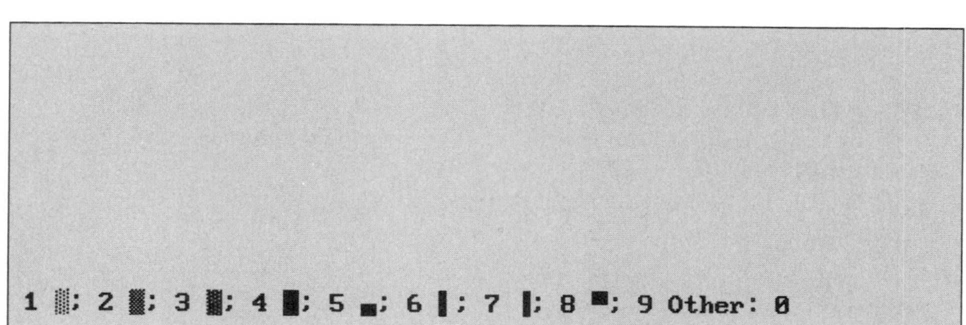

Figure 7–11
Additional Characters Used for Drawing

Option 1 draws single lines. Option 2 draws double lines. Option 3 draws lines with the asterisk (*) symbol. Option 4 gives you a new menu of characters from which you can choose (see fig. 7–11). Option 5 erases by moving the cursor through the drawing. Option 6 enables you to move the cursor around the screen without drawing or erasing lines.

7–10 DRAWING A BOX WITH SINGLE LINES

To draw a box with single lines, start with a clear screen. If the screen is not clear, press F7 and press N twice. Do the following:

1. Press Ctrl-F3 to display the Screen menu.
2. From this menu, select option 2 (Line Draw) to display the Line Draw menu.
3. From this menu, choose option 1 (Single Lines).
4. Press the right-arrow key 25 times. The status line should read:

```
Pos 3.5"
```

5. Press the Esc key. Your status line should read:

```
Repeat Value=8
```

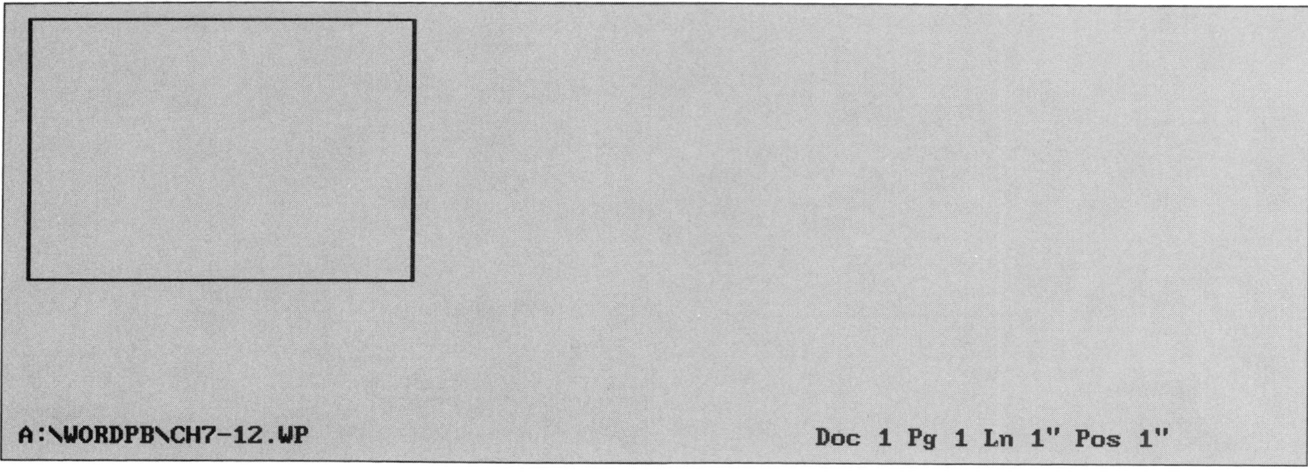

Figure 7–12
A Box with Single Lines

The default value 8 means that WordPerfect will draw the line in 8 lines or 8 positions. If you don't want this value, type your own value. For this example, we used 10.

6. Press the down-arrow key. WordPerfect moves down 10 lines and draws a single line.
7. Press Esc, type *25,* and press the left-arrow key. WordPerfect draws a line 25 positions long.
8. Press Esc, type *10,* and press the up arrow. Your box is complete (see fig. 7–12). Press 0 to return to the original screen.

The repeat option can be very helpful in drawing. Suppose that you want to separate two sections of a document with 60 dashes. Follow these steps:

1. Press Esc to turn on the Repeat mode. The status line reads:

```
Repeat Value=8
```

2. Enter the desired value.
3. Type the command or the character to be repeated.

The commands that can be repeated are the four arrow keys (left, right, down, and up), PgUp, PgDn, Ctrl-left arrow (which moves the cursor to the left one word), Ctrl-right arrow (which moves the cursor to the right one word), Ctrl-Backspace (which deletes a word), and Alt-F10 (to execute a macro).

7–11 DRAWING A BOX WITH SPECIAL SYMBOLS

In this exercise, we want to show you other symbols besides the single line. This time you want to draw a box in the middle of the screen. Do the following:

1. Move the cursor to line 2.5″ and position 3.0″.
2. Press Ctrl-F3 to display the Screen menu.
3. Choose option 2 (Line Draw).

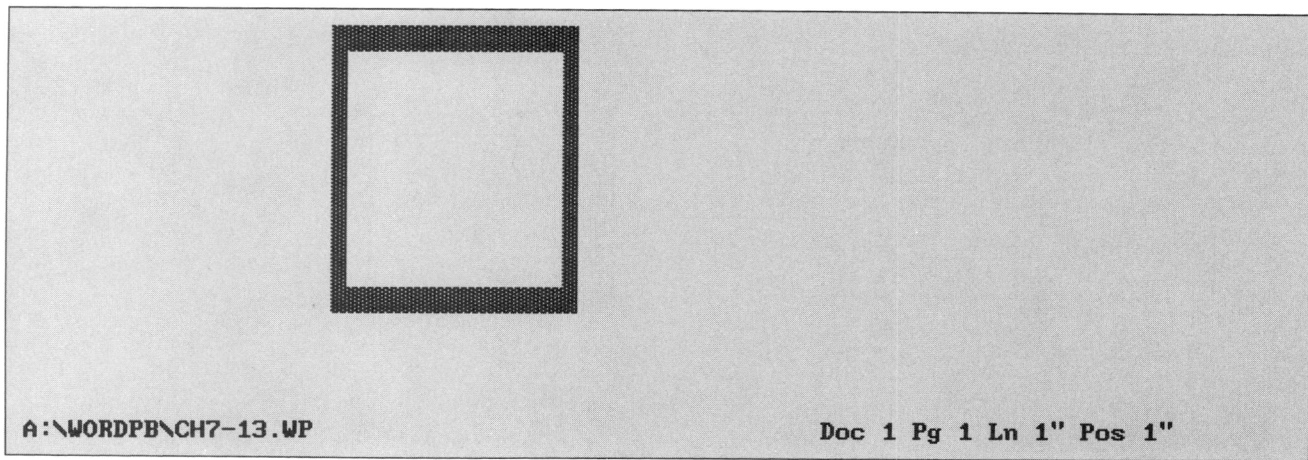

Figure 7–13
A Box Drawn with a Special Symbol

4. Select option 4 (Change). You will see the additional characters available (see fig. 7–11).
5. Select option 3. You are returned to the Line Draw menu and option 3 is changed from * to the special symbol you selected. Choose option 3 again; this symbol will stay in effect until you leave WordPerfect.
6. Move the cursor 15 positions to the right. The status line should read:

```
Pos 4.5"
```

7. Press Esc, type *10,* and press the down arrow. WordPerfect draws the line in 10 lines (10 vertical positions).
8. Press Esc, type *15,* and press the left arrow.
9. Press Esc, type *10,* and press the up arrow.

Now your box is complete (see fig. 7–13).

7–12 EDITING FEATURES OF THE LINE DRAW MENU

Option 5 (Erase) in the Line Draw menu will erase any portion of the figure you have created. Select this option and move the cursor in any direction, right, left, up, or down. You can use the Move command to move the cursor to any position on the screen without deleting the drawing.

7–13 DRAWING LINES AROUND TEXT

Suppose that you want to draw a box around each of the following words:

INPUT PROCESS OUTPUT

You also want to connect these boxes. Follow these steps:

1. Begin with a clear screen.
2. Move the cursor to line 2.5″ and Pos 2.0″. Type *INPUT*.

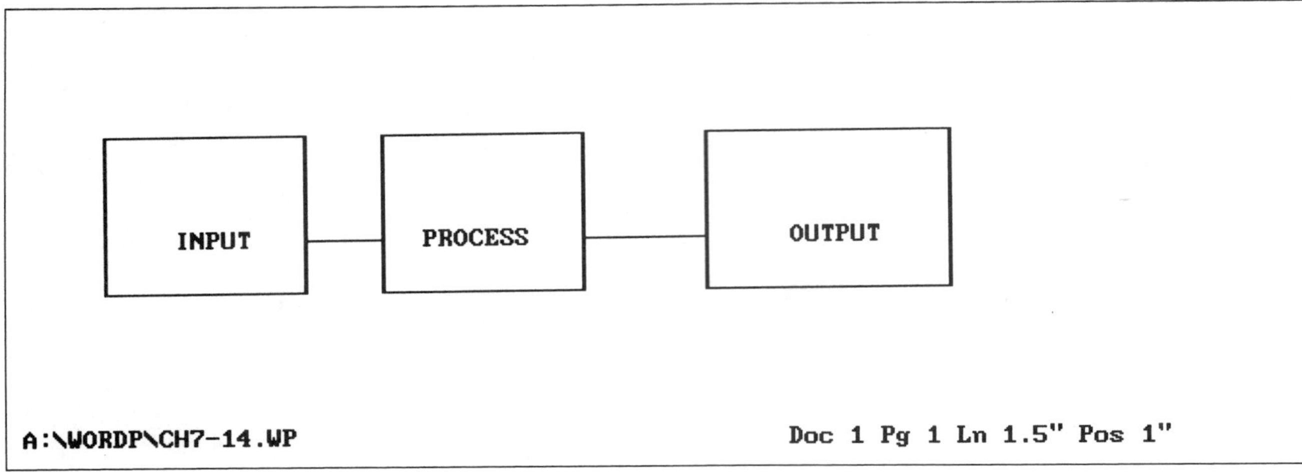

Figure 7–14
A Simple Structure Chart

3. Move the cursor to line 2.5″ and Pos 4.0″. Type *PROCESS*.
4. Move the cursor to line 2.5″ and Pos 6.0″. Type *OUTPUT*.
5. Move the cursor to line 2.5″ and position 1.5″.
6. Press Ctrl-F3 to display the Screen menu. Choose option 2 (Line Draw).
7. Select option 1 (Single Line).

We leave the rest of it to you. The final product is presented in figure 7–14.

7–14 PULL-DOWN MENU HIGHLIGHTS

1. To enter footnotes into your document, select Layout from the main menu. Choose Footnote or Endnote, and then choose Create.
2. To enter subscript or superscript, select Font from the main menu. From the Font menu, select Superscript or Subscript.
3. To perform sort operations, choose Tools from the main menu. Then select Sort, press Enter twice, and select the sort sequence.
4. To use the line drawing feature, pick Tools from the main menu, select Line Draw, and choose the drawing tool.

SUMMARY

This chapter reviewed four advanced features of WordPerfect: footnotes and endnotes, subscripts and superscripts, sort operations, and line drawing features. The first two features help you design scientific- and research-oriented documents. Sort operations are helpful for data-management tasks. The line-drawing features enable you to draw charts and boxes in your document.

REVIEW QUESTIONS

*These questions are answered in Appendix A.

1. What are footnotes? How are they created?

*2. What is the difference between footnotes and endnotes?

3. What are three commonly used formats for typing footnotes?
4. How do you display the Footnote menu?
*5. How do you exit the Footnote menu?
6. How do you edit an existing footnote?
7. What are the footnote options? What is the default option?
8. What are subscripts? Superscripts?
9. Why do you use superscripts? Subscripts?
*10. How do you display the Superscript/Subscript menu?
11. When you enter a subscript or superscript, is it displayed on-screen? If not, how do you know you have entered a subscript or superscript?
*12. How do you exit the Superscript/Subscript menu?
13. What are sort operations?
14. What is a primary key? A secondary key?
*15. How many sorting keys are allowed in WordPerfect?
16. What is the sort order?
17. What is an alphanumeric key?
*18. How do you display the Sort menu?
19. How do you exit the Sort menu?
20. How do you change the sort key?
21. How do you change the sort key type from numeric to alphanumeric?
22. What are some of the applications of the line drawing feature of WordPerfect?
23. How do you display the Line Draw menu?
24. How many symbols are available for drawing lines?
25. How do you erase a portion of a line?
26. What command is used for moving without erasing in Line Draw mode?
27. How do you draw a box?
28. What is the default value of the symbol for drawing?

HANDS-ON EXPERIENCE

1. In the following document, enter the three footnotes in the specified places. The text is as follows:

Because silicon technology is not able to emit light and has speed limitations, computer designers have concentrated on gallium arsenide technology. In gallium arsenide, electrons move almost five times faster than in silicon. Devices made with this synthetic compound can emit light, withstand higher temperatures, and survive much higher doses of radiation than silicon devices.[1]

The fifth-generation project in Japan has specified the following goals:[2]

- Listen when spoken to; then do what it is told
- Assist programming itself
- Sort through volumes of facts to find and use only what is pertinent

Teleshopping may also become a reality by incorporating other senses, such as touch, smell, and taste, into the telecommunication system.[3] For example, a consumer may be able to purchase an item by computer. The consumer may not only see the product but may also be able to touch and taste it as well.

The three footnotes are as follows:

> [1]John J. Posa, "Using Silicon and Gallium Arsenide," *High Technology,* March 1987, pp. 38–41.
>
> [2]Richard K. Miller, *Fifth Generation Computers* (Lilburn, GA: The Fairmount Press, Inc., 1987), p. 3.
>
> [3]Edward Cornish, "Did You Hear the One About the Human Who . . .?," *ComputerWord,* November 1986, pp. 28–29.

- **a.** Use the View Document command to see whether the footnotes are inserted properly.
- **b.** Edit the second footnote by changing the last name of the author to capital letters.
- **c.** Use option 4 of the Footnote menu to change the style of footnote 1 to a style of your choice.
- **d.** Change all footnotes to endnotes.

2. Using the subscripts option, enter the following equations:

$$X_1 + X_2 + X_3 + X_4 = a$$
$$X_1 - X_2 + 2X_3 - X_4 = b$$
$$2X_1 + X_2 - X_3 + 2X_4 = c$$
$$X_1 + 3X_2 + 5X_3 - 2X_4 = d$$

3. Using the superscripts option, enter the following text:

$$2^3 + 2^2 = 12$$
$$2^5 + 2^4 = 48$$

4. Set up the following table:

NAME	CREDIT	AGE
John	1000	39
Bob	500	50
Sue	700	61

- **a.** Sort this table by lines.
- **b.** Sort by age (in descending order).
- **c.** Sort first by age, and then by credit limit in ascending order.
- **d.** Sort this table by credit limit in ascending order.

5. Using the line drawing feature of WordPerfect, draw boxes around the following text:

Input

Process

Output

The boxes should also be connected vertically to one another.

6. Repeat Exercise 5 using a different symbol.

KEY TERMS

Ascending order
Descending order
Endnotes
Footnotes
Line drawing
Primary key
Secondary key
Sort operations
Subscripts
Superscripts

KEY COMMANDS

Turn on the Block feature (Alt-F4)

Display the Screen menu (Ctrl-F3)

Display the Footnote menu (Ctrl-F7)

Display the Superscript/Subscript menu (Ctrl-F8)

Display the Sort/Merge menu (Ctrl-F9)

Exit (F7)

Underline (F8)

Display the Print menu (Shift-F7)

MISCONCEPTIONS AND SOLUTIONS

Misconception You just finished drawing a box or boxes for one document and want to repeat the process for another document.

> **Solution** Using the Rectangle Block command, you can copy or move sections of your drawings to another document.

Misconception You try to display the Sort By Line menu by pressing Ctrl-F9. The following menu is displayed:

```
1 Merge; 2 Sort; 3 Convert Old Merge Codes:0
```

This does not seem to be the menu you want.

> **Solution** You may have forgotten to turn on the Block feature (Alt-F4). If the Block feature is on and the sort range is highlighted, press Ctrl-F9. You will see the Sort menu you want (see fig. 7– 7).

DIFFERENCES BETWEEN WORDPERFECT 4.2 AND 5.0

- In WordPerfect 4.2 you must press Shift-F1 to display the Superscript/Subscript menu. There are slight differences between this menu and the WordPerfect 5.0 menu.
- In WordPerfect 4.2, Tab Set and Tabs are options 1 and 2 in the Shift-F8 menu.
- In WordPerfect 4.2, when you press the Esc key, the message displayed is

```
n=8
```

DIFFERENCE BETWEEN WORDPERFECT 5.0 AND 5.1

- In WordPerfect 5.0, pressing Ctrl-F9 displays:

```
1 Merge; 2 Sort
```

ARE YOU READY TO MOVE ON?

Multiple Choice

1. The Footnote feature allows the following choices except
   a. create
   b. edit
   c. selecting the footnote format (APA, MLA, Turabian)
   d. choosing a new starting number
   e. selecting a numbering style
2. By default, the Font command (Ctrl-F8) allows
   a. superscripts
   b. subscripts
   c. special math symbols (such as the square root symbol)
   d. both a and b
   e. all of the above
3. After choosing the Font command, superscripts and subscripts are located on the
   a. Appearance option
   b. Size option
   c. Base Font option
   d. Base Color option
   e. none of the above
4. To perform sort operations, you must first decide
   a. how much of the document is to be sorted
   b. which key you want to use for the sort
   c. the manner in which to sort (ascending or descending)
   d. which sequence to use for the sort
   e. none of the above
5. If you sort a file first on the key LNAME, and then on the key FNAME, the key FNAME is known as the
   a. primary key
   b. secondary key
   c. major key
   d. minor key
   e. none of the above
6. If you want to create a box or draw simple charts, you should use WordPerfect's line drawing feature, which is found by pressing
   a. F5 (Text In/Out)
   b. Alt-F9 (Graphics)
   c. Alt-F5 (Mark Text)
   d. Ctrl-F3 (Screen)
   e. F6 (Bold)
7. Commands that can be repeated using the Esc key include
   a. the four arrow keys (up, down, left, right)
   b. PgUp
   c. PgDn
   d. Alt-F10 (Macro Execution)
   e. all of the above
8. By default, the first key used in WordPerfect's sort operation is

a. the first field
b. the last field
c. any numeric field
d. the field that contains the person's last name
e. none of the above

9. The Footnote menu enables you to select from all of the following except
   a. footnote
   b. text attributes (boldfaced or underlined, for example)
   c. endnote
   d. endnote placement
   e. none of the above
10. While in the line drawing feature, to place the cursor at another location on the screen without drawing lines, select the option
   a. *
   b. Change
   c. Erase
   d. Other
   e. Move

True/False

1. Features such as footnotes and endnotes, subscripts and superscripts, sort operations, and line drawing are considered advanced features of WordPerfect.
2. When using WordPerfect's footnote feature, footnotes are renumbered automatically if you make changes to them.
3. Once you create a footnote, you cannot edit it to make any changes.
4. WordPerfect does not support any data-management operations.
5. You must not include column headings within the block of data to be sorted.
6. WordPerfect cannot sort on more than one key.
7. WordPerfect's line drawing feature can draw only single lines; it cannot draw double lines or use other characters.
8. To draw a line 50 characters long, you can use the Esc key and set the repeat value to 50 once you are in the Line Draw menu.
9. The repeat function of the Esc key works only with Line Draw.
10. WordPerfect supports several numbering options for footnotes including numbers, letters, and characters.

ANSWERS

Multiple Choice

1. c
2. d
3. b
4. a
5. b
6. d
7. e
8. a
9. b
10. e

True/False

1. T
2. T
3. F
4. F
5. T
6. F
7. F
8. T
9. F
10. T

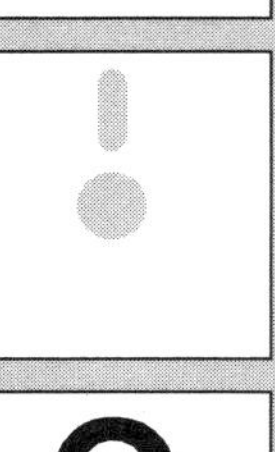

Using WordPerfect Advanced Features: Part II

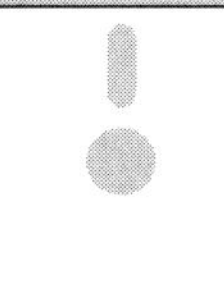
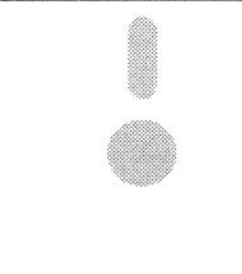

8–1 INTRODUCTION

In this chapter we discuss three advanced features of WordPerfect. These powerful features are outline creation for term papers and writing projects, macro design and use, and math operations. In the WordPerfect appendix, we introduce four additional advanced WordPerfect features, including desktop publishing, the equation editor, the spreadsheet, and table handling. These features make WordPerfect a true work companion for home and office.

8–2 OUTLINES

The **outline** feature of WordPerfect enables you to create outlines that are easy to use and modify. If you add or delete a number in the outline, the remaining numbers are updated automatically. Outlines are helpful for organizing your thoughts. You can set up a rough outline and as new ideas occur to you, you can enter them and WordPerfect will organize and renumber the outline for you.

Some word processing programs include a built-in outliner that can manipulate text. WordPerfect does not have such a feature, but the outliner feature included should handle the majority of your outlining requirements.

You use the outline feature to create numbered and indented outlines. An example of an outline is as follows:

I. Level one outline
   A. Level two outline
   B. Level two outline
   C. Level two outline
      1. Level three outline
      2. Level three outline
II. Level one outline
   A. Level two outline
   B. Level two outline

WordPerfect also allows you to generate numbered paragraphs.

8–2–1 Creating an Outline

The following outline shows a portion of a table of contents of a textbook:

I. Lotus Functions
   A. Financial Functions
      1. Present value
      2. Future value
   B. Statistical Functions
      1. Average
      2. Variance
II. Lotus Graphs
   A. Pie Charts
   B. Line Graphs

You can use WordPerfect to create this outline and modify it. Start with a clear screen and do the following:

1. Press Shift-F5 to turn the outline feature on.
2. From this menu select option 4 (Outline). This brings up the Outline menu. Select 1 for On. The status line reads Outline.
3. Press Enter to enter the first outline number (I).
4. Press the spacebar to move over one position.
5. Type *Lotus Functions,* and press Enter. Number II. will be displayed.
6. Press Tab. At this point number II. is changed to letter A. and is indented.
7. Press the spacebar to move the cursor by one space.
8. Type *Financial Functions.*
9. Press Enter. The letter B. is displayed.
10. Press Tab once. At this point letter B. is changed to 1. and is indented.
11. Press the spacebar. Type *Present Value.*
12. Press the Enter key. The number 2. is displayed.
13. Press the spacebar. Type *Future Value.*
14. Press the Enter key. The number 3. is displayed.
15. Move the cursor under the number 3. with the left-arrow key and then press backspace once. The number 3. is changed to the letter B.
16. Press the right-arrow key once to move the cursor to the right of the letter B., then press the spacebar once. Type *Statistical Functions.* Press Enter. The letter C. is displayed. Press Tab. The number 1. is displayed.
17. Press the spacebar. Type *Average.* Press Enter. The number 2. is displayed. Press the spacebar.
18. Type *Variance.* Press Enter. The number 3. is displayed.
19. Using the left-arrow key, move the cursor under the number 3. then press the backspace key twice. This will change the 3. to the number II. Press the right-arrow once to move the cursor to the right of number II.
20. Press the spacebar. Type *Lotus Graphics.* Press Enter. The number III. will be displayed. Press Tab. Number III. is changed to letter A. and will be indented. Press the spacebar.
21. Type *Pie Charts.* Press Enter. Letter B. will be displayed. Press the spacebar.
22. Type *Line Graphs.*

Your work should be similar to figure 8–1. Press Shift-F5 and select 4 (Outline), then select 2 to turn outline mode off. This may seem time-consuming, but do not forget when the outline is established modifications can be done easily.

If you want to add to your outline, first turn on the outline feature, and then move the cursor to the end of the line above the line where you want to make the insert. Press Enter. The cursor should be under the number that has appeared on the screen. If the insertion is not a level one entry, tab to the correct position with the Tab key. Press the spacebar and type your new entry.

To delete an outline heading, place the cursor on the heading you want to delete and use the Del key to erase it. WordPerfect automatically renumbers the remaining entries in the outline. You also can change the level number.

```
I. Lotus Functions
     A. Financial Functions
          1. Present Value
          2. Future Value
     B. Statistical Functions
          1. Average
          2. Variance
II. Lotus Graphics
     A. Pie Charts
     B. Line Graphs

A:\WORDPB\CH8-1.WP                                  Doc 1 Pg 1 Ln 2.83" Pos 1"
```

Figure 8–1
An Example of an Outline

8–2–2 Changing the Outline Numbering Format

WordPerfect allows different numbering formats for your outline. To change the format of the outline presented in figure 8–1 to legal format, do the following:

1. Retrieve the document.
2. Move the cursor to the beginning of the document and press Shift-F5 to display the Outline menu.
3. Choose option 6 (Define). The Paragraph Numbering Definition menu is displayed (see fig. 8–2).
4. From this menu, select option 4 (Legal Numbering).
5. Press Enter twice.
6. Use the arrow keys to move the cursor down through your outline. You will see that the numbering format is changed automatically. Figure 8–3 shows this new outline.

8–2–3 Numbering Paragraphs

WordPerfect's paragraph numbering feature can be very helpful. Suppose, for example, that you are writing about nine different authors in nine paragraphs. You could number these paragraphs, and then, if you want to move paragraph eight after paragraph two, the task will be simple.

```
Paragraph Number Definition

     1 - Starting Paragraph Number                1
           (in legal style)
                                                  Levels
                                   1     2     3     4     5     6     7     8
     2 - Paragraph                 1.    a.    i.   (1)   (a)   (i)    1)    a)
     3 - Outline                   I.    A.    1.    a.   (1)   (a)    i)    a)
     4 - Legal (1.1.1)             1    .1    .1    .1    .1    .1    .1    .1
     5 - Bullets                   •     o     -     ■     *     +     ·     x
     6 - User-defined

     Current Definition            I.    A.    1.    a.   (1)   (a)    i)    a)
     Attach Previous Level               No    No    No    No    No    No    No

     7 - Enter Inserts Paragraph Number           Yes

     8 - Automatically Adjust to Current Level    Yes

     9 - Outline Style Name




Selection: 0
```

Figure 8–2
The Paragraph Numbering Definition Menu

```
1 Lotus Functions
     1.1 Financial Functions
          1.1.1 Present Value
          1.1.2 Future Value
     1.2 Statistical Functions
          1.2.1 Average
          1.2.2 Variance
2 Lotus Graphics
     2.1 Pie Charts
     2.2 Line Graphs














A:\WORDPB\CH8-3.WP                                   Doc 1 Pg 1 Ln 2.83" Pos 1"
```

Figure 8–3
An Outline in Legal Style

```
I.   WordPerfect is one of the most popular word processing
programs on the market. The personnel office is planning to conduct
a brief seminar on this package.

II.  Tom Morris from the personnel office will be the instructor.
All the administrative staff are invited.

III. To encourage all of you to attend the seminar, there will be
cash prizes awarded to three participants.

IV.  After familiarizing yourselves with WordPerfect, all of you
who participate will be given access to a PC with WordPerfect
capabilities.






A:\WORDPB\CH8-4.WP                              Doc 1 Pg 1 Ln 1" Pos 1"
```

Figure 8–4
An Example of Numbered Paragraphs

If you have several paragraphs you want to number, first enter the text, and then do the following:

1. Move the cursor to the left of the paragraph you want to number.
2. Press Shift-F5 and choose option 5 (Para Num). On the status line you see:

```
Paragraph Level (Press Enter for Automatic):
```

3. Press Enter.

Continue this process until all your paragraphs are numbered. Figure 8–4 shows an example of numbered paragraphs. If you delete one of these paragraphs, WordPerfect automatically renumbers the rest.

8–3 WORDPERFECT MACRO OPERATIONS

The majority of WordPerfect operations are performed by a series of keystrokes. These keystrokes can be recorded and then played back by using a **macro.** Whenever you have a repetitive task to perform, you should consider creating a macro. In addition to simplifying the task, macros can lessen the chance of making a mistake.

You can run a WordPerfect macro in batch mode or in interactive mode. In **batch mode,** the macro is executed from beginning to end without user intervention. In an **interactive mode,** the user is able to enter certain keystrokes during macro execution.

Developing a Macro 8–3–1

In general, macro creation follows these steps:

1. Begin macro recording.
2. Name the macro. The name can be similar to a file name, with up to eight characters, or you can use Alt in combination with a letter of the alphabet, A through Z.
3. Describe the macro.
4. Enter the desired keystrokes.
5. Stop recording.
6. Execute the macro. The macro can be executed anywhere on the screen. However, you should execute the macro in an area that does not include any text; otherwise it will overwrite the present text.

Creating a Macro 8–3–2

Suppose that you always sign all your business letters as follows:

Sincerely yours,

Tom Johnson, Ph.D.
Director
Management Information Systems Dept.

Because you type this same information time and time again, it is a good candidate for a macro. To design a macro to enter this information for you, do the following:

1. Start with a blank screen.
2. Press Ctrl-F10 to turn on the recording feature. The status line will say:

```
Define macro:
```

   Type *Finish* for the macro name and press Enter.
3. The status line will say:

```
Description:
```

   Type a brief description for your macro and press Enter. In this case, type *closing*.
4. The status line flashes the message:

```
Macro Def
```

   Type *Sincerely yours,* and press Enter four times to insert three blank lines.
5. Type *Tom Johnson, Ph.D.* and press Enter.
6. Type *Director* and press Enter.
7. Type *Management Information Systems Dept.* and press Enter.
8. Press Ctrl-F10 to turn off the recording mode. The status line will stop flashing.

```
Sincerely Yours,


Tom Johnson, Ph.D.
Director
Management Information Systems Dept.











A:\WORDPB\CH8-5.WP                          Doc 1 Pg 1 Ln 1.33" Pos 1"
```

Figure 8–5
A Sample Macro

This macro is saved on the default drive with the extension WPM. You can specify a drive other than the default when you specify the macro name. You can see this macro in figure 8–5.

8–3–3 Macro Execution

To execute the macro that you have just created, move the cursor to a blank area of the screen and press Alt-F10. The status line will say:

```
Macro:
```

Type *Finish* and press Enter. The macro is executed immediately, and you can see the result on-screen.

8–3–4 Editing a Macro

To edit your macro, you first must retrieve it by pressing Ctrl-F10. At the status line Define Macro: prompt, type the name of your macro and press Enter. The status line will show:

```
Finish.WPM Already Exists: 1 Replace; 2 Edit; 3 Description: 0
```

Option 1 allows you to replace the macro. If you select the Replace option, WordPerfect asks you for a new description—you are starting from scratch to build a new macro.

If you select the Edit option, WordPerfect displays the Edit menu (see fig. 8–6). Select option 1 from this menu to change the description of the macro. Enter a new description if you want, and then press Enter. Your changes will be saved automatically. To change the action of the macro (its function) select option 2. Option 2 puts you inside the action box. Make the changes you want,

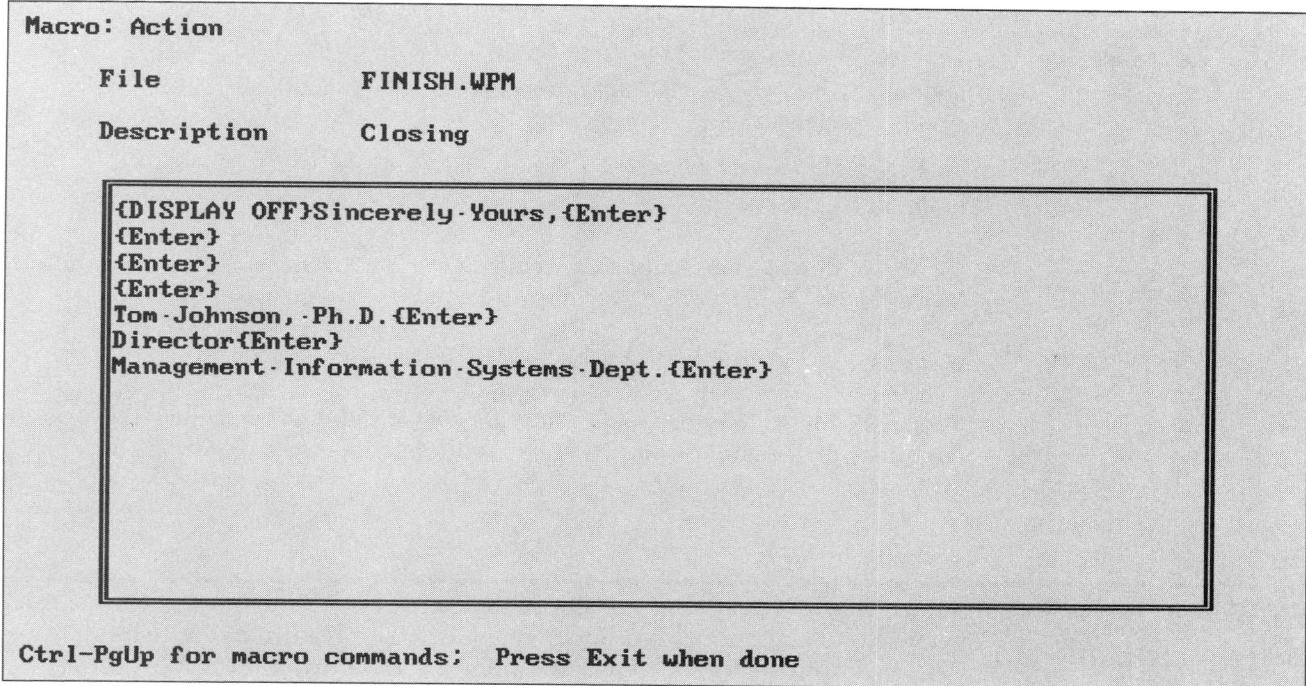
Macro: Action

File FINISH.WPM

Description Closing

{DISPLAY OFF}Sincerely·Yours,{Enter}
{Enter}
{Enter}
{Enter}
Tom·Johnson,·Ph.D.{Enter}
Director{Enter}
Management·Information·Systems·Dept.{Enter}

Ctrl-PgUp for macro commands; Press Exit when done

Figure 8–6
The Edit Menu

and then press F7 to save them. If you don't want to save your changes, press F1 to cancel.

An Interactive Macro 8–3–5

Often a macro will include a few keystrokes that must be changed every time the macro is executed. WordPerfect offers an interactive feature, which allows keyboard input during macro execution. To make a macro interactive, do the following:

1. Place the cursor where you want to insert keyboard input and press Ctrl-PgUp. The following menu will be displayed:

```
1 Pause; 2 Display; 3 Assign; 4 Comment: 0
```

2. Select option 1 and press Enter. The Macro Def indicator will flash.

When you execute the macro, it will pause for you to type your message. Press Enter to continue macro execution.

To demonstrate this feature, suppose that you want to keep all the information in the closing macro shown in figure 8–5, but you want to change the name every time you execute the macro. Follow these steps:

1. Start with a blank screen and press Ctrl-F10.
2. At the status line Define Macro: prompt, type *A:Keyboard* (the macro name) and press Enter.

3. At the status line Description: prompt, type *interactive* and press Enter.
4. Type *Sincerely yours,* and press Enter four times.
5. Press Ctrl-PgUp, select Pause, and press Enter two times.
6. Type *Director* and press Enter.
7. Type *Management Information Systems Dept.* and press Enter.
8. Press Ctrl-F10.

To invoke the macro, press Alt-F10, type *A:Keyboard,* and press Enter. WordPerfect displays

```
Sincerely yours,
```

and waits for your entry. Type *Mary Brown, MS* and press Enter. The macro continues to execute, displaying the rest of your message.

8–4 WORDPERFECT MATH FEATURES

WordPerfect offers some limited math features that you can use to calculate totals, subtotals, grand totals, and percentages. This feature can be helpful if you are dealing with tables that include numbers requiring these types of calculations.

You also can use these calculations to perform what-if analysis—change one of the values in your table, and other table values are calculated automatically. (Also see the discussion of WordPerfect's spreadsheet capability in the appendix.)

To use WordPerfect's math features, you must observe the following conventions:

- Positive numbers are entered with or without the plus sign (+), for example, 5 or +5.
- Negative numbers must be preceded by a minus sign (−) or they must be enclosed in parentheses, for example, −5 or (5).
- Commas can be used as separators for thousands, millions, and so forth or they can be left out, for example, 1,000,000 or 1000000.
- Percentages are entered as decimals or with a percent sign, for example, .5 or 50%.
- Use a lowercase "t" to indicate subtotals, for example, t200.
- Use an uppercase "T" to indicate totals, for example, T200.
- Numbers can include up to four decimal places.
- You can define a table up to 24 columns wide (columns A through X).
- WordPerfect's default is that the first column is a nonnumeric column reserved for headings and labels.
- You can select up to four columns as calculation columns, (for percentages, multiplication, exponentiation, and so on).
- To calculate subtotals, totals, and grand totals, select a numeric column.
- When you want to include descriptions and labels, select a nonnumeric column.

Math Operation Codes 8–4–1

There are three **math codes** that are commonly used with math operations. They are + to calculate a subtotal, = to calculate a total, and * to calculate a grand total.

Math Operation Formulas 8–4–2

WordPerfect uses four special formulas that can be used when defining a calculation column. They include + to add numbers in numeric columns, +/ to average numbers in numeric columns, = to add numbers in total columns, and =/ to average numbers in total columns.

Using Math Features to Complete a Table 8–4–3

To show how the math features of WordPerfect work, we have extracted a portion of the financial statement from the Northwest Textile Company. For simplicity, these numbers have been summarized in figure 8–7. We would like to use WordPerfect's math features to fill out all the empty cells in this figure. They include two subtotals in locations *a* and *b*, a total in location *c*, and a grand total in location *d*. We will be using column B for percentages. We leave column C for you to use for projection purposes. Column C is calculated as column A multiplied by .20 (A*.20). Follow these steps:

1. Start with a clear screen.
2. Press Shift-F8 (Format) to display the Format menu.
3. Press 1 or L (Line) to enter the Format: Line menu.
4. Select option 8 or T (Tab Set). The tab ruler will be displayed.
5. Press Home-left arrow to move the cursor to the left edge of the tab ruler (position −1″).

Sales	
North	100
South	200
East	300
West	400
Total Sales	a
Costs	
North	(50)
South	(120)
East	(200)
West	(250)
Total Costs	b
Net Income	c
Royalty	500
Grand Total	d

Figure 8–7
Northwest Textile Company Financial Statement

6. Press Ctrl-End to delete all the existing tab stops.
7. Press T (Type) to display the Tab Type menu.
8. Press 1 or A (Absolute) to select absolute as the tab type.
9. Type *2.5,3 Enter, 6.5 Enter* to set tabs at 2.5″, 5.5″ and 6.5″.
10. Press F7 (Exit) two times to return to document editing mode.
11. Press Alt-F7 (Columns/Tables).
12. Press 3 or M (Math).
13. Press 3 or D (Define) to display the Math Definition screen.
14. Type *1* to set column A up as a text column.
15. Press F7 (Exit) to exit the Math Definition screen.
16. Press 1 or O (On) to turn the Math feature on. You should now see the word "Math" in the lower-left corner of the screen.
17. Type *Sales,* then press Enter two times.
18. Press the Tab key then type *North.*
19. Press the Tab key again. You should now be in position 5.5″. This is your first numeric column. If you are in the right column the status line will indicate **"Align char = . Math"** in the lower-left corner of the screen. If this sign is not displayed you may be in the wrong column.
20. Type *100* followed by Enter. Repeat this process for South, East, and West, each with its respective amount. When you press Enter after typing the last sales amount, the cursor should be positioned at the far left of the page.
21. Type *Total Sales.*

```
Sales

               North                      100
               South                      200
               East                       300
               West                       400
Total Sales                             1,000.00+

Costs

               North                       (50)
               South                      (120)
               East                       (200)
               West                       (250)
Total Costs                               (620.00)+

Net Income                                 380.00=

Royalty                                   T500

Grand Total                                880.00*


                                                      Doc 1 Pg 1 Ln 1" Pos 1"
```

Figure 8–8
A Table with Subtotals, Totals, and Grand Totals

22. Press the Tab key two times (you should now be in position 5.5″) then type a "+" (plus) sign. This symbol will tell WordPerfect to include all of the above numbers when it calculates the table.
23. Press the Enter key two times, then continue entering the table as shown in figure 8–7. Be sure to type another "+" (in position 5.5″) when you get to the "Total Costs" line.
24. For the "Net Income" line, type an "=" in position 5.5″. This tells WordPerfect to add the totals calculated above into a subtotal.
25. For the "Royalty" line, type a "T" to the left of the amount (e.g., T500). This tells WordPerfect to add the Royalty amount into the Grand Total as a separate amount.
26. For the "Grand Total" line, type a "*" (in position 5.5″). This tells WordPerfect to add the subtotals and other amounts calculated above into a grand total. You are now ready to calculate the document.
27. Press Alt-F7 (Columns/Tables).
28. Press 3 or M (Math).
29. Press 4 or C (Calculate). WordPerfect will automatically calculate your table. If everything is correct, your grand total should be $880.00.

Your screen should look like the one shown in figure 8–8.

Defining a Calculation Column 8–4–4

As mentioned earlier, WordPerfect allows you to define up to four **calculation columns.** We would like to define the second numeric column, column B, as the percentage column. This means that every number in column A will be divided by the grand total. Do the following:

1. Press the Home key three times, and then press the up arrow to move the cursor to the top of the document above any code. Note that the word Math must not show in the lower-left corner of the screen.
2. Press F2 (Search) to enter the search mode. WordPerfect will display "→ Srch:" in the lower-left corner of the screen.
3. Press Alt-F7 (Columns/Tables).
4. Press 3 or M (Math).
5. Press 3 or D (Def). WordPerfect will now display [Math Def] as the search string.
6. Press F2 (Search) to initiate the search. WordPerfect will find your existing math definition code, and will position the cursor immediately after it in the document.
7. Press Alt-F7 (Columns/Tables).
8. Press 3 or M (Math).
9. Press 3 or D (Define) to display the Math Definition screen. (See figure 8–9.)
10. Press the right arrow two times so that the cursor is in column C.
11. Type "0" to specify a calculation column. WordPerfect will automatically move the cursor to the calculation section of the screen. You are now ready to enter the formula that you will use for the calculation.

```
Math Definition             Use arrow keys to position cursor

Columns                     A B C D E F G H I J K L M N O P Q R S T U V W X

Type                        2 2 2 2 2 2 2 2 2 2 2 2 2 2 2 2 2 2 2 2 2 2 2 2

Negative Numbers            ( ( ( ( ( ( ( ( ( ( ( ( ( ( ( ( ( ( ( ( ( ( ( (

Number of Digits to         2 2 2 2 2 2 2 2 2 2 2 2 2 2 2 2 2 2 2 2 2 2 2 2
  the Right (0-4)

Calculation    1
  Formulas     2
               3
               4

Type of Column:
      0 = Calculation    1 = Text     2 = Numeric    3 = Total

Negative Numbers
      ( = Parentheses (50.00)         - = Minus Sign  -50.00


Press Exit when done
```

Figure 8–9
Math Definition Screen

```
Sales

               North                       100          0.11!
               South                       200          0.23!
               East                        300          0.34!
               West                        400          0.45!
Total Sales                              1,000.00       1.14!

Costs

               North                       (50)        (0.06)!
               South                      (120)        (0.14)!
               East                       (200)        (0.23)!
               West                       (250)        (0.28)!
Total Costs                               (620.00)     (0.70)!

Net Income                                 380.00       0.43!

Royalty                                   T500          0.57!

Grand Total                                880.00       1.00!


A:\WORDP\8-8.WP                          Doc 1 Pg 1 Ln 1" POS 1"
```

Figure 8–10
A Table with One Calculation Column

12. Type *B/880* followed by Enter. This means that every item in column B will be divided by 880 (the grand total).
13. Press F7 (Exit) to return to the Math menu.
14. Press 0 to return to document editing mode.
15. To calculate the result, move the cursor to the immediate right of each number. Press the Tab key to move to column C. You will see an exclamation mark (!), and the status indicator reads "Align char = . Math". The Math On feature must be in effect). Press the down-arrow key then the Tab key to create the exclamation mark for the next number and continue this for all the other numbers. Remove the calculation symbols (+, =, *) that were used to generate the Total Sales, Total Costs, Net Income, and Grand Total. If you do not do this, WordPerfect will not calculate the percentages for these fields.
16. Press Alt-F7 (Columns/Tables).
17. Press 3 or M (Math).
18. Press 4 or C (Calculate). The resulting document is presented in figure 8–10.

8–5 PULL-DOWN MENU HIGHLIGHTS

1. To create outlines, select Tools from the main menu. From the Tools menu select Outline, and then press Enter to turn the outline feature on.
2. To number paragraphs, from the main menu select Tools and then Paragraph Number. Press Enter to accept the default paragraph level.
3. To turn the recording feature on, from the main menu select Tools. From this menu select Macro, and then select Define. Specify a macro name and a description.
4. To execute a macro, select Macro from the main menu. Next, choose Execute and specify a macro name.
5. To invoke the math feature, from the main menu select Layout. Choose Math and press Enter to turn the math feature on.

SUMMARY

In this chapter we explained the outline feature of WordPerfect. Using this feature you will be able to set up outlines for term papers and easily revise these outlines. We also discussed WordPerfect's macro capability. With macros, you can simplify repetitive tasks to improve both the efficiency and the accuracy of your work. The last features discussed in the chapter were math operations. Using these operations, you can perform simple math calculations such as totals, subtotals, and percentages.

REVIEW QUESTIONS

*These questions are answered in Appendix A.

1. What is an outline?
2. What capabilities are provided by the outline feature of WordPerfect?
3. When the outline is finished, can you modify it?
*4. How do you get the outline feature started?
5. How do you change the outline numbering?

6. How many different numbering formats are available in the outline feature?
7. How do you number paragraphs?
*8. What is a macro?
9. What are some of the applications of macros?
10. What are the steps in developing a macro?
11. How do you get the macro recording mode started?
*12. How do you stop the recording operation?
13. How do you execute a macro?
14. What is the convention in naming a macro?
15. How do you edit a macro?
16. What is the Pause feature in macro design?
17. What is the purpose of the Display command in an interactive macro?
18. What is an interactive macro?
19. How do you stop a macro while it is being executed?
20. What is the math feature of WordPerfect?
*21. How do you get the math feature started?
22. How many columns can be defined?
*23. By default, is the first column numeric or nonnumeric?
24. How many calculation columns can be defined?
25. How do you know if a column has been defined as a calculation column?
26. What are the codes used with the math feature?

HANDS-ON EXPERIENCE

1. Using the outline feature of WordPerfect, set up the following outline:

```
  I. Word Processing Major Functions
     A. Document Creation
     B. Cut/Paste
     C. Merge Printing
     D. Macro Design
 II. Spreadsheet Major Functions
     A. What-If Analysis
     B. Graphics Analysis
     C. Financial and Statistical Analysis
III. Database Management Functions
     A. Search Operations
        1. Single Criterion Search
        2. Multiple Criteria Search
     B. Sort Operations
        1. Numeric Sort
        2. Nonnumeric Sort
```

2. Change this outline to legal format.
3. Design a macro to print the following:

   Dear Classmates,
   We all have learned so much about WordPerfect.

4. Design an interactive macro to insert the name for the following closing:

Sincerely yours,

Any Name, Ph.D.
Marketing Director

Remember that the name will be entered during macro execution.

5. Using the math features of WordPerfect, design the following table:

Sales	
Region 1	100
Region 2	200
Total Sales	a
Expenses	
Region 1	−50
Region 2	−75
Total Expenses	b
Net Income	c
Other Income	300
Grand Total	d

a. Calculate subtotals, totals, and the grand total.

b. Set up a calculation column (column B) to project these figures for the next period by multiplying column A by .17.

KEY TERMS

Batch mode
Calculation columns
Interactive mode
Macro
Math codes
Outline

KEY COMMANDS

Display the Math menu (Alt-F7)

Retrieve a macro (Alt-F10)

Display the Screen menu (Ctrl-F3)

Enter a pause in a macro (Ctrl-PgUp)

Turn on the macro recording feature (Ctrl-F10)

Indent (F4)

Exit (F7)

Turn on the outline feature (Shift-F5)

Display the Line Format menu (Shift-F8)

MISCONCEPTION AND SOLUTION

Misconception You set up your math table and perform calculations, but your calculations seem to be incorrect.

Solution Try widening your columns. Most probably your numbers overlap, which results in incorrect calculations.

DIFFERENCES BETWEEN WORDPERFECT 4.2 AND 5.0

- In WordPerfect 4.2 to turn the outline feature on you must press Alt-F5.
- In WordPerfect 4.2 to number a paragraph, first you must press Alt-F5 then select option 2 from this menu. In WordPerfect 4.2 the prompt after this option is

```
Para#
```

- In WordPerfect 4.2, the file extension for a macro is MAC.
- Debugging a macro in WordPerfect 4.2 is different from WordPerfect 5.0.
- In WordPerfect 4.2 the prompt in math operations is

```
Align char=.
```

DIFFERENCES BETWEEN WORDPERFECT 5.0 AND 5.1

- The Outline menu in WordPerfect 5.0 is slightly different from the one in WordPerfect 5.1.
- When you are editing a macro in WordPerfect 5.0, the prompt on the status line is slightly different than the one in WordPerfect 5.1.
- The procedure for setting tabs in WordPerfect 5.1 is different from the one in WordPerfect 5.0.

ARE YOU READY TO MOVE ON?

Multiple Choice

1. To turn on the outline feature, press
   - **a.** Shift-F5
   - **b.** Shift-F10
   - **c.** Alt-F10
   - **d.** Ctrl-F10
   - **e.** none of the above
2. WordPerfect macros are good candidates for all of the following except
   - **a.** to type a fixed heading
   - **b.** to type a fixed closing
   - **c.** to type an address
   - **d.** to type a term paper
   - **e.** all of the above
3. A macro name is
   - **a.** similar to a file name (it can have up to eight characters)
   - **b.** composed of Alt and a letter A through Z
   - **c.** both a and b
   - **d.** only letters A through H
   - **e.** only names similar to file names
4. To turn off the macro recording feature, you must press
   - **a.** Alt-F5
   - **b.** Ctrl-F10
   - **c.** Enter

- **d.** Esc
- **e.** none of the above

5. To execute a macro, type
- **a.** the macro name when the cursor is flashing
- **b.** Alt-F9
- **c.** Alt-F5
- **d.** any of the above
- **e.** Alt-F10 first, then the macro name

6. WordPerfect's math feature does all of the following except
- **a.** totals
- **b.** subtotals
- **c.** grand total
- **d.** line graphs of the growth
- **e.** percentages

7. WordPerfect's math feature allows up to how many columns for calculation?
- **a.** 4
- **b.** 3
- **c.** 2
- **d.** 1
- **e.** 5

8. WordPerfect's math feature allows numbers with up to how many decimal places?
- **a.** 1
- **b.** 4
- **c.** 2
- **d.** 3
- **e.** 5

9. To start the math feature (after your tabs are set), you must first press
- **a.** Shift-F8
- **b.** Shift-F5
- **c.** Alt-F7
- **d.** Alt-F5
- **e.** Ctrl-F5

10. To define a calculation column, you must
- **a.** see "Math" in the status line
- **b.** see "Math Def"
- **c.** see the Block feature indicator flashing
- **d.** see a + sign in the status line
- **e.** not see "Math" in the status line

True/False

1. WordPerfect includes a built-in outliner program.

2. To turn on the outline feature in WordPerfect, you must first press Shift-F5.

3. To turn off the outline feature, you must press Shift-F8.

4. Legal numbering is not one of the options in numbering paragraphs or outlines.

5. To turn on the macro recording feature, you must press Ctrl-F10.

6. WordPerfect offers editing features for macros.
7. You cannot pause an interactive macro for keyboard entry.
8. The editing menu for macros displays the macro function and all the codes.
9. The T and t have special meaning in WordPerfect when used with math operations.
10. In math operations, the first column is always numeric.

ANSWERS

Multiple Choice

1. a
2. d
3. c
4. b
5. e
6. d
7. a
8. b
9. c
10. e

True/False

1. F
2. T
3. F
4. F
5. T
6. T
7. F
8. T
9. T
10. F

Appendix A
WordPerfect 5.1

A–1
WORDPERFECT 5.1: A QUICK REVIEW

In WordPerfect 5.1 it is easy to create tables, print mailing labels, import spreadsheets, and print complex equations. There is a pull-down menu that can be used with or without a mouse, and the Help facility has been improved.

Pull-Down Menus and Mouse Support

In addition to the traditional function key access to features, WordPerfect 5.1 includes pull-down menus and mouse support. The pull-down menus are accessible with a single key. You can quickly proceed through the feature menus by typing the highlighted letter of each menu option or by moving to the option using the arrow keys. You can use the mouse not only for feature selection, but also for moving the cursor and blocking text.

Columns

The Columns feature is ideal for writing a newsletter, glossary, script, or any text that requires a columnar format. You can create up to 24 newspaper-style (snaking) or parallel (side-by-side) columns at any point in your document. Parallel columns can extend beyond a page break, which is especially convenient for script writing. Spacing can be changed within a column.

Tables/Spreadsheets

The Tables feature lets you easily create up to 32,765 rows and 32 columns of tabular data automatically enclosed in graphic lines. You can perform math functions on the numeric data in a table, and import spreadsheets into a table or anywhere else in WordPerfect.

Specifications

WordPerfect supports over 450 dot-matrix, daisy wheel, and laser printers and the number continues to grow. WordPerfect 5.1 also includes PostScript support. For details about each printer and its capabilities when using WordPerfect, contact WordPerfect Corporation's Information Services Department.

The DOS version of WordPerfect 5.1 runs on the IBM PC, XT, AT, PS/2, and true compatibles. The program requires 384K of "free memory." More system memory, including expanded memory, will improve the program's performance. Two 720K (or larger) floppy disk drives are required (a hard disk is recommended). A graphics adapter and matching monitor are required for displaying graphics features.

Versions of WordPerfect are also available for Data General and VAX minicomputers, Apple IIe/IIc, Apple IIGS, Macintosh, Amiga, and Atari computers, and for computers running under the UNIX/XENIX operating systems. WordPerfect 5.1 runs on a stand-alone PC or on a network.

Speller/Thesaurus/Hyphenation

The WordPerfect 115,000-word Speller is one of the largest integrated spellers on the market. It examines documents for spelling and typographical errors, as well as for unintentional double words. The Thesaurus (10,000 headwords) can be used to find synonyms and antonyms for specific words in a document or for individual words typed from the keyboard. Hyphenation is now dictionary-based, making it more accurate.

Printing

WordPerfect supports over 450 dot-matrix, daisy wheel, and laser printers. You can set up WordPerfect so that measurements are displayed in inches, centimeters, or points, whether you're setting margins, tabs, or spacing. With WordPerfect 5.1 (and supported printers that print graphics), you can directly print any of the more than 1,700 characters in the WordPerfect character sets—characters like Greek letters and trademark, copyright, and math symbols.

Labels

Mailing labels are easy to print with WordPerfect 5.1. Simply specify the dimensions of your labels and the number of labels on each page, and your printing will be perfect. You can define a format for each type of mailing label you use.

Equations

WordPerfect 5.1 includes an Equation Editor so that you can easily print scientific and technical formulas and equations. The editor includes a comprehensive collection of symbols, characters, and mathematical operators and functions. With the Equation Editor, you can enter an expression and immediately preview its printed appearance.

Figure A–1 shows the WordPerfect 5.1 command map. Following the command map, we review four of the most impressive improvements of WordPerfect 5.1 over its earlier releases.

A–2 DESKTOP PUBLISHING

The Graphics key adds a desktop-publishing dimension to WordPerfect. Using graphics in your work can help you produce professional presentation-quality documents.

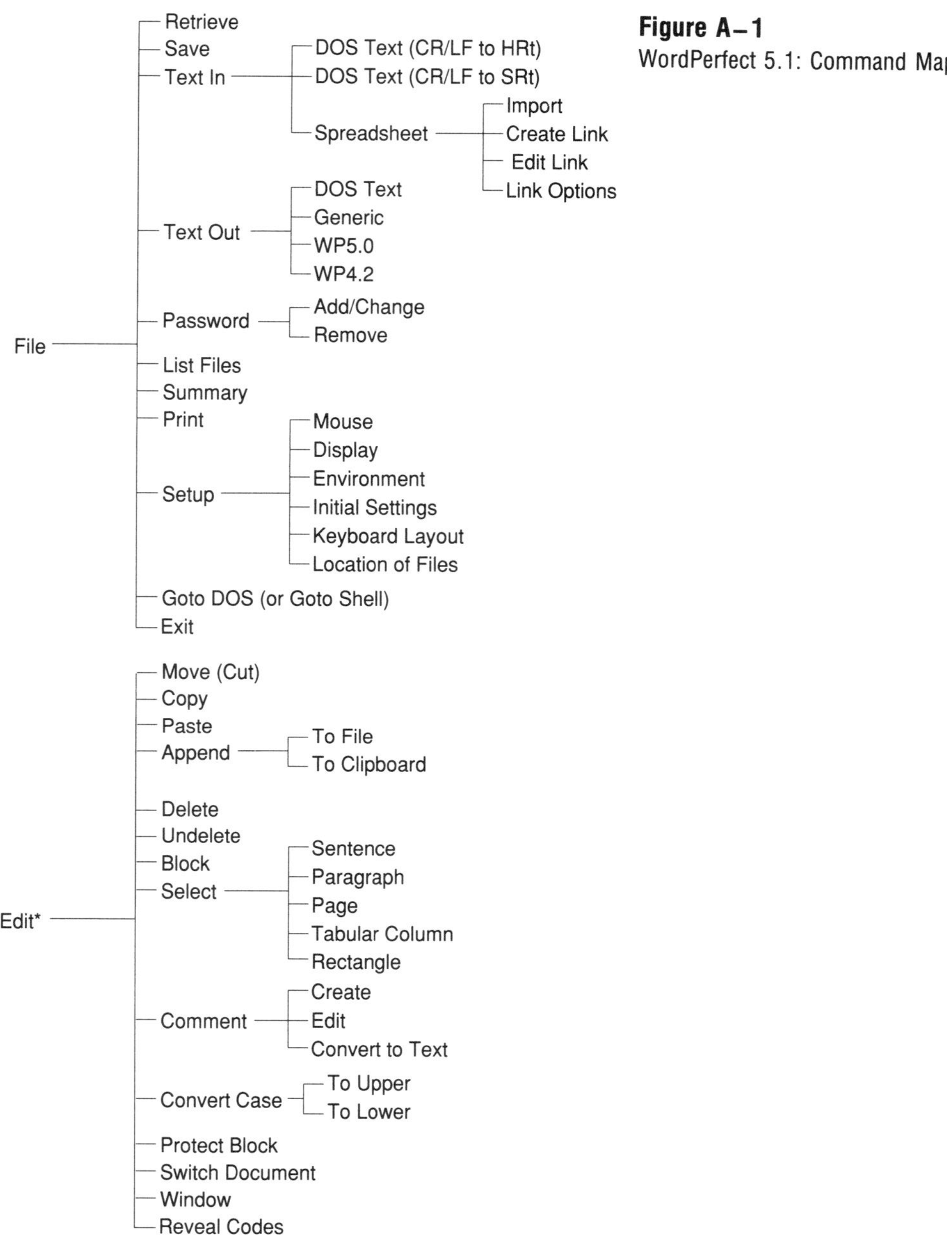

Figure A–1
WordPerfect 5.1: Command Map

Begin by pressing the Alt-F9 (Graphics) key. WordPerfect responds by presenting the Graphics menu as follows:

```
1 Figure; 2 Table Box; 3 Text Box; 4 User Box; 5 Line; 6 Equation: 0
```

The Figure, Table Box, Text Box, and User Box options are all essentially identical, so we will discuss only the Figure option. Each type of box

Figure A–1 *(Continued)*

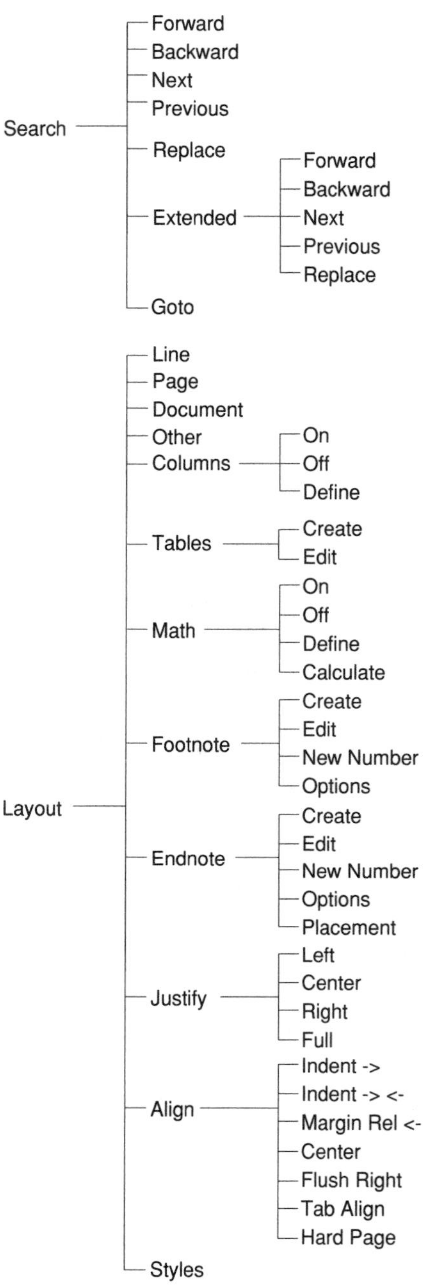

is numbered separately by WordPerfect, and each can have its own default option settings without affecting any of the other types of boxes.

Choose option 1 to enter the Figure menu. The Figure menu is as follows:

```
Figure: 1 Create; 2 Edit; 3 New Number; 4 Options: 0
```

The Create option allows you to create graphics boxes of all kinds. You can enter text, graphics images, footnotes, and many other types of data into a graphics box, and you can use different fonts. When you choose the Create option, the options shown in table A–1 are available.

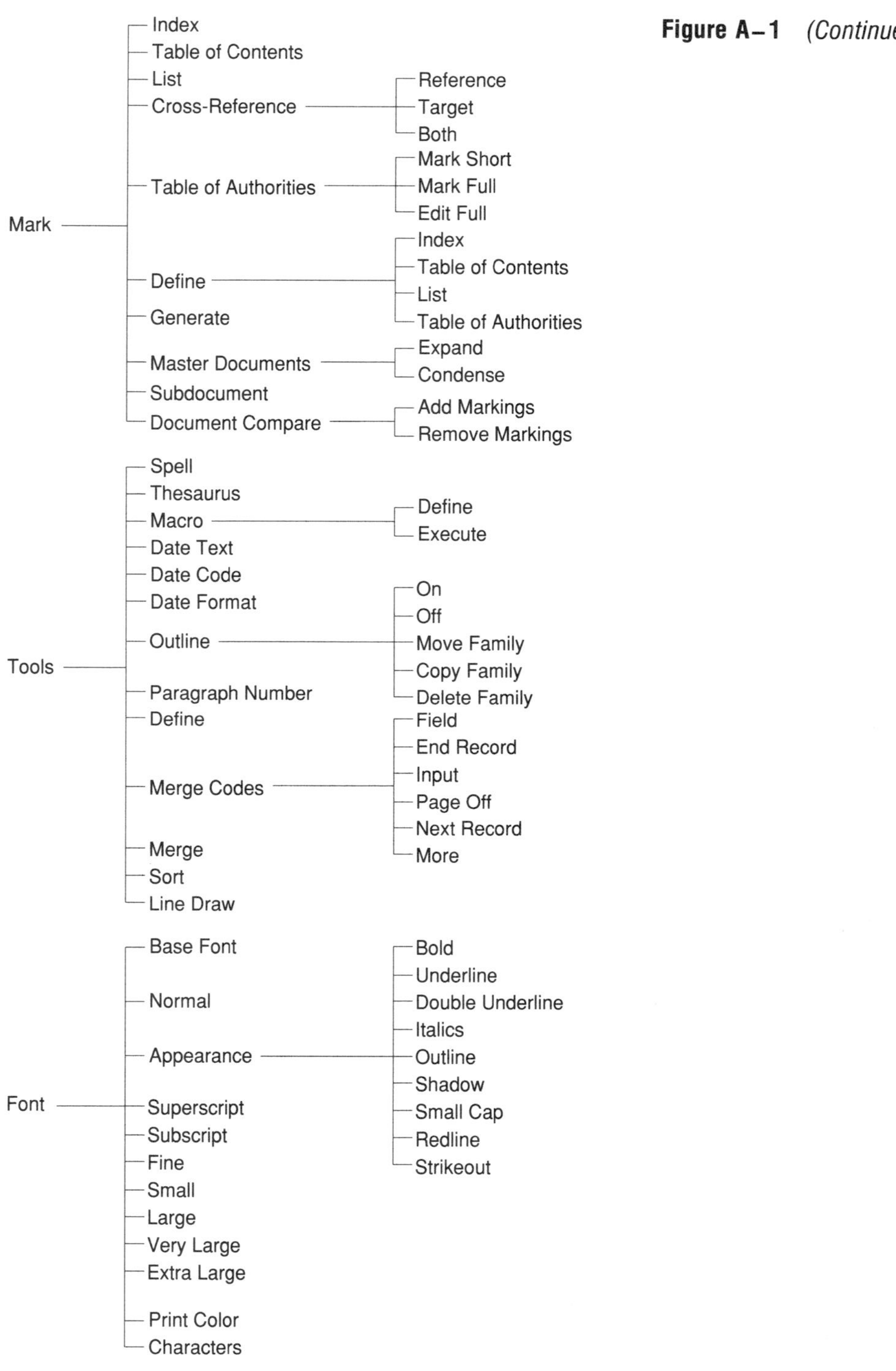

Figure A–1 *(Continued)*

Begin with a clear screen and follow these steps:

1. Press Alt-F9 (Graphics).
2. Press 1 or F to enter the Figure menu.
3. Press 4 or 0 to enter the Options menu.
4. Press 1 or B to specify the Border Style.

Figure A–1 *(Continued)*

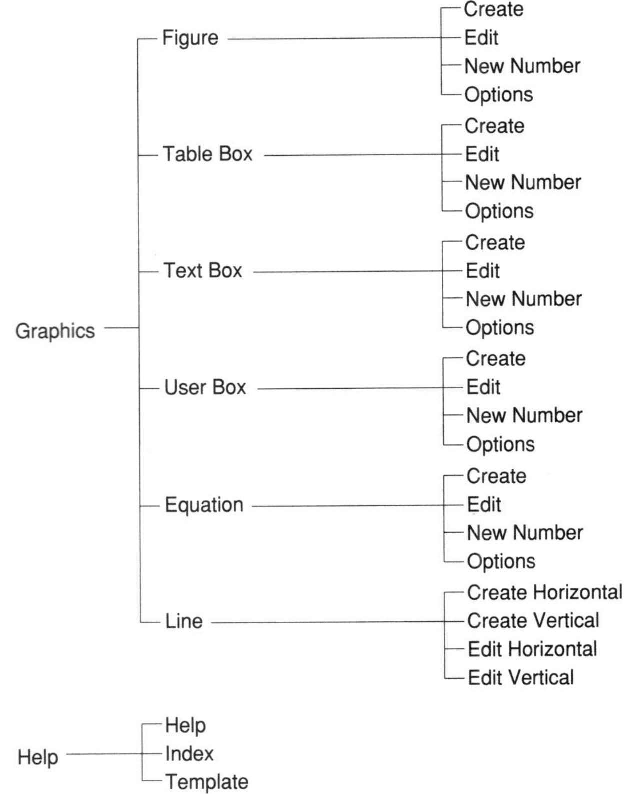

5. Type *SSSS* to specify the single-line borders.
6. Press 2 or 0 to specify the Outside Border Space.
7. Type *.167* and press Enter at each of the four prompts.
8. Select 3 or I to specify the Inside Border Space.
9. Type *.167* and press Enter at each of the four prompts.
10. Select 9 or G to select the Gray Shading (% of Black) option.
11. Type *0* and press Enter to specify no gray shading.
12. Press Enter to exit.

Next, do the following:

1. Press Alt-F9.
2. Select 1 or F to enter the Figure menu.
3. Select 1 or C to create a new figure.
4. Select 1 or F to specify a file name. WordPerfect supplies 30 graphics files with each package of WordPerfect 5.1. We are assuming that these graphics files are located in the current (default) subdirectory.
5. Type *BUTTRFLY.WPG* to specify the name of one of the graphics files that WordPerfect supplies. WordPerfect will look in the default directory for this file.
6. Select 6 or H to enter the Horizontal Position of the graphics image.
7. Select 3 or C to center the graphics box on the page.

Table A–1
Options Under Create

1-Filename	By selecting this option, you can specify a file to import into the Figure box. The file can contain text, graphics images, or equations. It is worth noting that WordPerfect supplies a sample of graphics images in each package. These files are identified by the extension WPG, and can usually be found in the WP51 subdirectory.
2-Contents	Allows you to tell WordPerfect whether the contents of the Figure box will be graphics, text, or equations.
3-Caption	Using this option, you can create your own caption for the graphics box.
4-Anchor Type	The Anchor Type option presents its own submenu as follows:
Paragraph	Choosing this option will tell WordPerfect to keep the graphics box with the current paragraph. If the paragraph is moved to a new location, the graphics box will go with it.
Page	Choosing the Page option tells WordPerfect to keep the graphics box on the current page, regardless of the movement of surrounding text.
Character	This option tells WordPerfect to regard the graphics box as a single character. This allows WordPerfect to position the next line of text below the bottom of the graphics box.
5-Vertical Position	Using this option, you can adjust the vertical positioning of the graphics box on the page.
6-Horizontal Position	This option allows you to control the horizontal positioning of the graphics box on the page.
7-Size	The Size option allows you to adjust the vertical (height) and horizontal (width) size of the box. The Size submenu is as follows:
Set Width/Auto Height	This option allows you to specify the width as a static number, and tells WordPerfect to adjust the height as needed.
Set Height/Auto Width	This option allows you to specify the height as a static number, and tells WordPerfect to adjust the width as needed.
Set Both	This option allows you to specify both the width and the height as static numbers.
Auto Both	This option allows WordPerfect to determine the natural width and height of the graphics box, adjusting to the contents as required.
8-Wrap Text Around Box	If set to "Yes," then surrounding text will flow around the graphics box, filling empty space to the left or right of the graphics box. If this option is set to "No," then text flow will be turned off and will resume immediately below the graphics box.
9-Edit	This option allows you to edit the contents of the graphics box. Recall that there are no real differences between the different types of boxes. However, it is important to note that the type of box selected at the "Contents" prompt will tell WordPerfect which editor to retrieve. WordPerfect can then use the editor that is best suited to the contents of the graphics box. The three editors available are the Text Editor, the Graphics Editor, and the Equation Editor.

Figure A–2
A Graphics Example

8. Press 7 or S to enter the size menu.
9. Press 1 or W to specify Width/Auto Height.
10. Type *6.5* and press Enter to specify the new width.
11. Press Enter to return to document editing mode.
12. Press Shift-F7 (Print).
13. Select 2 or P to print the page.

You will see a figure similar to figure A–2. When you are finished reviewing and working with the graphics image, clear the screen. To do this, press F7, and choose No, No.

A–3
TABLE CREATION AND MANIPULATION

WordPerfect 5.1 now offers an elegant and sophisticated table-handling and creation capability. Tables can be used for a variety of purposes, including handling data in a spreadsheet mode, creating calendars, and designing forms.

Tables are useful for creating forms that have a tabular, row-and-column format. A table can be described as a set of rows and columns of information. The rows run horizontally across the table, and the columns run vertically. Up to 32 columns and 32,765 rows can be specified in the table. The intersection of any row with any column is called a "cell." Calendars, spreadsheet data, and forms are all very easy to create and maintain using tables in WordPerfect.

To create a table, press Alt-F7 (Columns/Tables). The following options will be displayed:

```
1 Columns; 2 Tables; 3 Math: 0
```

Select option 2 (Tables), and WordPerfect asks whether you want to Create (option 1) or Edit (option 2) a table. Choose option 1 (Create). WordPerfect next asks you how many columns will be in the new table. Type *4* and press Enter to tell WordPerfect that you want 4 columns in the table. Next, WordPerfect wants to know how many rows you want in the table. Type *4* and press Enter. WordPerfect creates the table with 4 rows and 4 columns, and you are placed in the table-editing screen. The table-editing options are as follows:

Ctrl-arrow key	Pressing the Ctrl key along with any of the arrow keys enables you to expand or contract the size of the cell the cursor is in.
Ins	Press the Insert key to insert rows or columns into the table.
Del	Press the Delete key to delete rows or columns from the table.
Move	Press Ctrl-F4 (Move/Copy) to move or copy rows or columns within the table.
Size	Enables you to change the number of rows or columns in the table.
Format	Displays a submenu, as follows:
Cell	By default, WordPerfect regards all cells in the table as numeric for calculation purposes. You can also define a cell as "text." Cell attributes, justification, and vertical alignment can also be defined here. Finally, the Cell format option allows you to "lock" the contents of the cell so that the contents cannot be altered from the normal document editing screen. This is useful for entering titles, column headers, and so on.
Column	The Column format option allows you to specify column widths and attributes, justification, and number of digits to the right of the decimal point (up to a maximum of 15).
Row Height	The Row Height format option allows you to specify how many lines of text can be entered into each cell, and whether or not the table will expand as text is entered into the cell.
Lines	Enables you to change the appearance of the lines used to create the table. Cell shading can also be specified with this key.

Header	If the table is more than 1 page in length, the Header option enables you to specify what information will appear in the cells that print at the top of each consecutive page.
Math	Choosing the Math option displays the following submenu:
Calculate	This option tells WordPerfect to recalculate all the formulas in the table.
Formula	Allows you to create formulas referencing other cells in the table.
Copy Formula	Allows you to copy formulas to new areas of the table. WordPerfect table formulas are relative, meaning that the formula will change its cell references according to its current position in the table.
+	This option tells WordPerfect to add all of the cells directly above the function to a subtotal.
=	This option tells WordPerfect to add all of the subtotals directly above the function to a total.
*	This option tells WordPerfect to add all of the totals directly above the function to a grand total.
Options	This option allows you to adjust text spacing inside cells and to control the display of negative data and the horizontal position of the table on the page.
Join	The Join option allows adjacent cells (rows or columns) in the table to be joined into a single, larger cell.
Split	The Split option allows single cells to be split apart into sub-cells (rows or columns).

The WordPerfect cursor occupies the entire upper left corner of the table (cell A1). You can reposition the cursor by pressing any of the arrow keys, moving the cursor in the direction indicated. Press the F7 (Exit) key to exit the table-editing mode. Experiment with arrow keys to move the cursor around in the table. When you are finished practicing cursor movement, move the cursor back to the upper left corner of the table, and then type *Table handling in WordPerfect is fun and easy.*

As you can see, the size of the row that the cursor is in adjusts to accommodate the text entered. Text automatically wraps to the next line when it reaches the right margin of the current cell. Press the Backspace key to erase the text you just entered.

Next, you will build a sample spreadsheet using formulas. To do this, make sure that the cursor is in the upper left corner of the table (cell A1), then follow the following steps.

1. Press Alt-F7 to enter Table Edit mode.
2. Press Alt-F4 or F12 (Block) to turn on the Block feature.
3. Press the right-arrow key three times, and then press the down-arrow key three times to highlight the entire table.
4. Press 2 or F (Format) to enter the Format menu.
5. Press 1 or C (Cell) to enter the Cell menu.
6. Press 3 or J (Justify) to enter the Justification menu.
7. Press 2 or C (Center) to tell WordPerfect to center all the entries in the table.
8. Press F7 (Exit) to exit Table Edit mode.
9. Press the up arrow three times, and then press the left arrow three times to move the cursor to the upper left corner of the table (cell A1).
10. Type the following information and press the keys indicated:

Type	Press
REGION	right arrow
QUARTER 1	right arrow
QUARTER 2	right arrow
TOTALS	down arrow once, and left arrow three times
WEST	right arrow
51,200	right arrow
57,550	down arrow once, and left arrow twice
EAST	right arrow
49,250	right arrow
54,600	down arrow once, and left arrow twice
GRAND TOTAL	right arrow three times, and up arrow twice

11. Press Alt-F7 (Columns/Tables).

    Notice that WordPerfect automatically places you in Table Edit mode.
12. Press 5 or M (Math).
13. Press 2 or F (Formula).
14. Type *B2+C2* and press Enter.

    WordPerfect automatically calculates the total of cell B2 plus cell C2.
15. Press the down-arrow key.
16. Press 5 or M (Math).
17. Press 2 or F (Formula).
18. Type *B3+C3* and press Enter.

    The total is calculated.
19. Press the down-arrow key.
20. Press 5 or M (Math).
21. Press 4 or +.

    WordPerfect automatically calculates the total of the cells immediately above the cursor, and places the total in the lower-right cell (D4).
22. Press the left-arrow key.
23. Press Alt-F4 or F12 (Block) to turn on the Block feature.
24. Press the left-arrow key twice to highlight the first three cells of the fourth row.

REGION	QUARTER 1	QUARTER 2	TOTALS
WEST	51,200	57,550	108,750.00
EAST	49,250	54,600	103,850.00
GRAND TOTAL			212,600.00

Figure A–3
A Sample Table Using WordPerfect

25. Press 7 or J (Join) to join the highlighted cells.
26. Press Y to tell WordPerfect that you want to join the highlighted cells. WordPerfect automatically joins them, and adjusts "GRAND TOTAL" to its new position.
27. Press the F7 (Exit) key to exit Table Edit mode.
28. Press Shift-F7 (Print).
29. Select 2 or P to print the table.

When you are finished with the table, clear the screen by pressing F7 (Exit), N, and N.

Your final product should be similar to figure A–3. As you can see, table-handling in WordPerfect is easy and fun. You can perform just about any desired operation within a WordPerfect table. Text, graphics, and numeric data can be mixed into the table to create spreadsheets, forms, calendars, reports, and so forth. A little practice is all it takes to become proficient with the new Table feature in WordPerfect.

A–4
SPREADSHEET HANDLING

To access the Spreadsheet menu, press Ctrl-F5 (Text In/Out). WordPerfect responds with the following options:

```
1 DOS Text; 2 Password; 3 Save As; 4 Comment; 5 Spreadsheet: 0
```

Choose option 5 or S (Spreadsheet) from this menu to display the Spreadsheet submenu as follows:

```
Spreadsheet: 1 Import; 2 Create Link; 3 Edit Link; 4 Link Options: 0
```

Using WordPerfect's spreadsheet link capabilities, you can easily import Lotus 1-2-3, Quattro, Quattro Pro, Excel, and PlanPerfect spreadsheet data into your documents. The spreadsheet options can be used as follows:

Import	Choosing this option enables you to import spreadsheet data directly from a spreadsheet file. A submenu is displayed, and the options presented are as follows:
1-Filename	Allows you to specify the name of the spreadsheet to be imported. The drive and full pathname of the file must be specified, including the three-character extension of the file name.
2-Range	Allows you to select the specific range of cells to import from the specified spreadsheet.
3-Type	Allows you to tell WordPerfect to handle the incoming data in Table mode or Text mode. See the discussion in the table-handling section for an explanation of the Type feature.
4-Perform Link	Choose this option to perform the actual link. WordPerfect attempts to find the specified file, locates the cell range, and imports the data into a new table in your document at the current cursor position.
Create Link	This option has the same submenu as the Import option. However, the Create Link option places beginning and ending link codes around the spreadsheet import table so that the linked spreadsheet can be easily imported at any time.
Edit Link	Allows you to modify any of the settings that were established using the Create Link option.
Link Options	The following options are contained under this option:
1-Update on Retrieve	Tells WordPerfect whether to perform the spreadsheet data import every time the document is called into memory.
2-Show Link Codes	By default, WordPerfect displays link comments on the

	screen in normal document editing mode. Set this option to No to suppress the display of link codes and comments. The codes/comments will still be visible through the Reveal Codes screen.
3-Update All Links	Tells WordPerfect to update all spreadsheet links in the current document.

Exit back to a clear screen, then follow these steps for an example of spreadsheet linking:

1. Press Ctrl-F8 (Font).
2. Press 1 (Size) and 3 (Fine) to tell WordPerfect to import the spreadsheet using the "Fine" character size attribute.
3. Press Ctrl-F5 (Text In/Out).
4. Press 5 or S to enter the Spreadsheet menu.
5. Press 2 or C to enter the Create Link menu.
6. Press 1 or F to specify a file name. We assume that you have a Lotus 1-2-3 file called CH24-1.WK1 located in the default directory (the same directory that you are working in).
7. Type *CH24-1.WK1* and press Enter to specify the file name.
   Notice that WordPerfect automatically "sensed" the proper range to pull in. If you do not specify a range, WordPerfect assumes that you want to import the entire spreadsheet.
8. Press 4 or P to perform the link.
   WordPerfect will go out to the disk, search for the file you have specified, and bring the spreadsheet data into the document. The spreadsheet data will be in table form, with link codes above and below the table. The sentence in the upper left corner of this spreadsheet is cut off. Use View Document mode, and the final printout will correctly show the entire contents of the cell.
9. Press Shift-F7 (Print).
10. Press 2 or P to print the page.
11. Clear the screen by pressing F7 (Exit), N, and N.

The spreadsheet-linking capabilities of WordPerfect enable you to establish, maintain, modify, and perform spreadsheet file and range imports in your documents. This means that you will no longer have to retype the spreadsheet data into your documents, and will eliminate the possibility of data-entry error. Using data imported directly from your favorite spreadsheet program, you can easily support findings and conclusions in your reports, documents, presentations, newsletters, memos, term papers, and personal letters.

A–5
EQUATION EDITOR

Using the equation editing capabilities of WordPerfect, you can create impressive documents that incorporate scientific, mathematical, engineering, Greek, and many other characters.

You can generate any character with the equation editor and print it with no problem. The equation editor converts the characters that you enter into "graphics." This means that WordPerfect no longer regards the characters as text but rather regards them as graphics. Printers can easily handle graphics characters because the printer doesn't have to be told how to generate the character's shape. The printer simply assumes that characters in graphics mode are graphics images, and handles them as such. For this reason, you no longer have to worry whether your printer will be able to handle the special character or symbol you want to print. To access the equation editor, press the Graphics key (Alt-F9). The following options are presented:

```
1 Figure; 2 Table Box; 3 Text Box; 4 User Box; 5 Line; 6 Equation: 0
```

Choose option 6 (Equation) and you are presented with the following options:

```
Equation: 1 Create; 2 Edit; 3 New Number; 4 Options
```

Choose option 1 (Create) and you will see the options shown in figure A–4. From this menu, choose option 9 (Edit). You will see the equation screen (see fig. A–5).

```
Definition: Equation

     1 - Filename

     2 - Contents               Equation

     3 - Caption

     4 - Anchor Type            Paragraph

     5 - Vertical Position      0"

     6 - Horizontal Position    Full

     7 - Size                   6.5" wide x 0.333" (high)

     8 - Wrap Text Around Box   Yes

     9 - Edit



Selection: 0
```

Figure A–4
Options Under Create

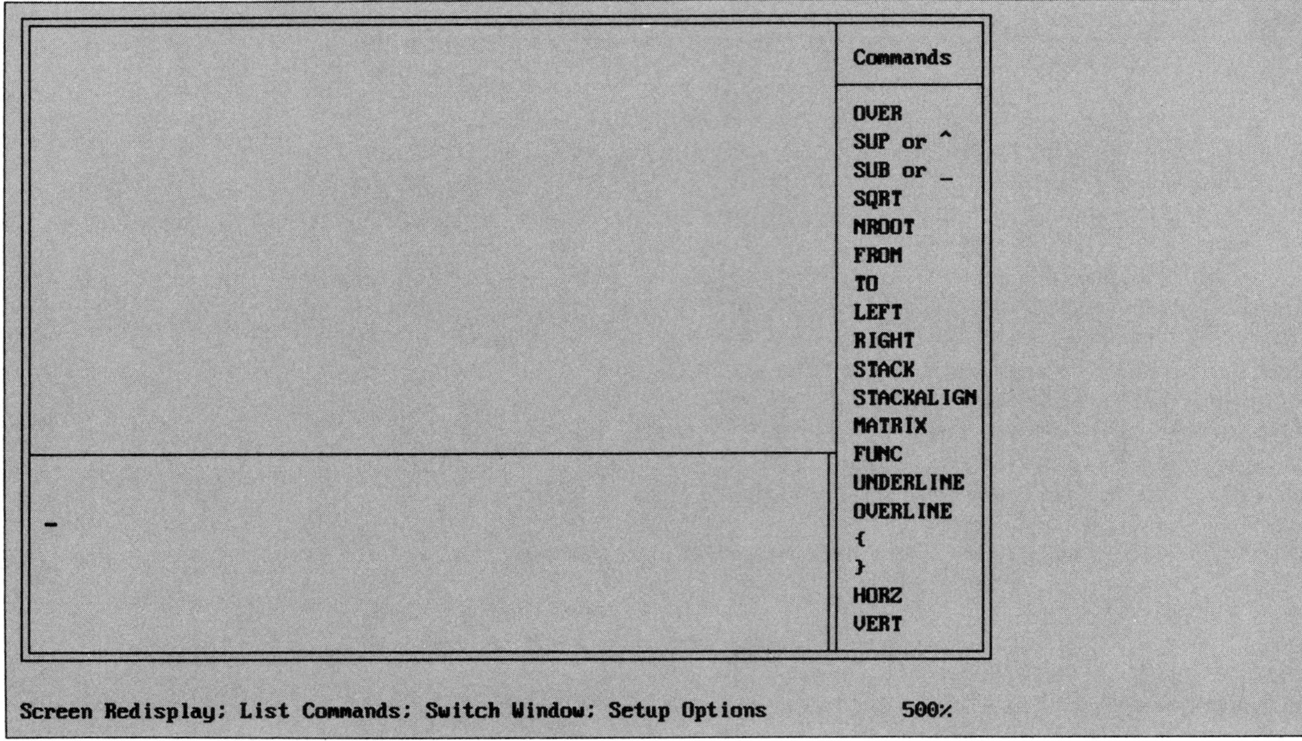

Figure A–5
Equation Screen

The equation screen is divided into three distinct areas. The large open area in the upper left corner is called the display window. This is where the equations, symbols, and characters that you enter are displayed. The tall area along the right edge of the screen is called the equation palette. From this palette, you can choose from many different characters and symbols. Finally, the area in the lower left corner is called the editing window. This is where you will do the work of creating special characters and equations. The cursor is waiting in the upper left corner of the editing window for your next command.

Once in the equation screen, you can choose any of the following options:

`Screen Redisplay   List Commands   Switch Window   Setup Options`

The following is an explanation of these commands:

Command	Function
Screen Redisplay	Performed by pressing the F9 function key, this command tells WordPerfect to display in the display window whatever you have entered into the editing window.

List Commands	Performed by pressing the List Files key (F5), this option tells WordPerfect to reposition the cursor into the equation palette. You can then use the arrow keys to move the cursor highlight bar to any symbol in the palette. Use the PgDn and PgUp keys to display other equation palettes to select the right character or symbol for the job. Press Enter at any symbol to move the cursor and the symbol or command into the editing window. Repeat the process to continue building the equation.
Switch Window	Performed by pressing the Switch key (Shift-F3), this option tells WordPerfect to reposition the cursor into the display window of the equation editor screen. You can then scale the characters to another size, rotate them, or move them to achieve the desired effect.
Setup Options	Performed by pressing the Setup key (Shift-F1) (see fig. A–6). The Print As Graphics op-

```
Equation: Options

     1 - Print as Graphics    Yes

     2 - Graphical Font Size  Default

     3 - Horizontal Alignment Center

     4 - Vertical Alignment   Center




Selection: 0
```

Figure A–6
Options Under the Setup Key (Shift-F1)

$$X = \frac{-B \pm \sqrt{B^2 - (4*A*C)}}{2*A}$$

Figure A–7
An Example of the Equation Editor

tion tells WordPerfect whether to handle the character as a graphics image or a text character. Graphical Font Size tells WordPerfect what size to print the character or symbol. Horizontal Alignment tells WordPerfect where on the line to print the equation. Valid options for Horizontal Alignment include Left, Center, and Right. The Vertical Alignment option tells WordPerfect where on the page to print the characters, symbols, or equation. Valid options include Top, Center, and Bottom. To exit from this menu, press F7.

Let's try an example. Your cursor should still be in the editing window. Follow these steps:

1. Type the following text:

   X = {−B PLUSMINUS SQRT{B SUP 2 − (4*A*C)}} OVER {2*A}

   We are trying to display the quadratic equation. PLUSMINUS stands for plus or minus, SQRT stands for square root, SUP stands for "to power," and OVER means division.

2. Press the F9 (Display) key. You have entered the quadratic formula. The text that you typed is automatically converted to an equation in the display window, showing what your printer will generate when these characters are passed to it. The equation editor allows you to enter and even "typeset" mathematical equations, symbols, and characters, but it doesn't calculate the results of the equations for you.
3. Press F7 (Exit), then press the space bar to return to document-editing mode.
4. Press Shift-F7 (Print).
5. Press 2 or P to print the equation.
6. When you are finished working with the equation editor, clear the screen by pressing F7 (Exit), N, and N. See figure A–7.

A–6
WORDPERFECT 5.0 COMMAND SUMMARY

Feature	Keystrokes
Advance	Shift-F8, 4, 1
Appearance Attributes	Ctrl-F8, 2

Automatic Reference	Alt-F5, 1
Automatically Format & Rewrite	Shift-F1, 3, 1
Backspace	
Backup	Backspace (←)
Base Font	Shift-F1, 1
Beep Options	Ctrl-F8, 4
Binding	Shift-F1, 5, 1
	Shift-F7, B or Shift-F1, 5, 7, 1
Block	Alt-F4 or F12
Block Protect (Block on)	Shift-F8
Bold	F6 or Ctrl-F8, 2, 1
^C (Text from Keyboard)	Shift-F9, C
Cancel	F1
Cancel Print Job	Shift-F7, 4, 1
Cartridges and Fonts	Shift-F7, S, 3, 5
Case Conversion (Block on)	Shift-F3
Center	Shift-F6
Center Page Top to Bottom	Shift-F8, 2, 1
Colors/Fonts/Attributes	Shift-F1, 3, 2
Columns (Text and Parallel)	Alt-F7
Compose	Ctrl-2 or Ctrl-V
Concordance	Alt-F5, 5, 3
Conditional End of Page	Shift-F8, 4, 2
Control Printer	Shift-F7, 4
Copy File	F5, ↵, 8
Create Directory	F5, =, Enter new directory name, Enter
^D (Date)	Shift-F9, D
Date	
Code	Shift-F5, 2
Format	Shift-F5, 3
Text	Shift-F5, 1
Date/Outline	Shift-F5
Decimal/Align Character	Shift-F8, 4, 3
Define (Mark Text)	Alt-F5, 5
Delete	
Character Left	Backspace
Character Right	Del
Directory	F5, ↵, 2
File	F5, ↵, 2
to End of Line (EOL)	Ctrl-End
to End of Page (EOP)	Ctrl-PgDn
Word	Ctrl-Backspace
Word Left	Home, Backspace
Word Right	Home, Delete
Display All Print Jobs	Shift-F7, 4, 3
Display Pitch	Shift-F8, 3, 1
Display Setup	Shift-F1, 3
Document Comments	Ctrl-F5, 5
Document Compare	Alt-F5, 6, 2

Document Format	Shift-F8, 3
Document Summary	Shift-F8, 3, 4
DOS Text File	
Retrieve (CR/LF to [HRt])	Ctrl-F5, 1, 2
Retrieve (CR/LF to [SFt])	Ctrl-F5, 1, 3
Save	Ctrl-F5, 1, 1
Double Underline	Ctrl-F8, 2, 3
^E (End of Record)	Shift-F9, E
Edit Table of Authorities	
Full Form	Alt-F5, 5, 5
Endnote	Ctrl-F7, 2
Endnote Placement Code	Ctrl-F7, 3
Enter	Enter
Exit	F7
Extra Large Print	Ctrl-F8, 1, 7
^F (Field)	Shift-F9, F
Fast Save	Shift-F1, 4
Figure (Graphics)	Alt-F9, 1
Filename on Status Line	Shift-F1, 3, 4
Fine Print	Ctrl-F8, 1, 3
Flush Right	Alt-F6
Footers	Shift-F8, 2, 4
Footnote	Ctrl-F7, 1
Force Odd/Even Page	Shift-F8, 2, 2
Format	Shift-F8
Forms	Shift-F7, S, 3, 4
^G (Start Macro)	Shift-F9, G
Generate (Mark Text)	Alt-F5, 6
Generate Tables, Indexes, etc.	Alt-F5, 6, 5
Generic Word Processor Format	Ctrl-F5, 3
"Go" (Start Printer)	Shift-F7, 4, 4
Go to DOS	Ctrl-F1, 1
Graphics	Alt-F9
Graphics Quality	Shift-F7, G
Graphics Screen Type	Shift-F1, 3, 5
Hard	
Page	Ctrl-Enter
Return	Enter
Return Display Character	Shift-F1, 3, 6
Space	Home, Space Bar
Headers	Shift-F8, 2, 3
Help	F3
Home	Home
Horizontal Line (Graphics)	Alt-F9, 5, 1
Hyphenation	Shift-F8, 1, 1
Hyphenation Zone	Shift-F8, 1, 2
→Indent	F4
→Indent←	Shift-F4

Index	
Define	Alt-F5, 5, 3
Mark	Alt-F5, 3
Initial Settings (Format)	Shift-F8, 3, 2
Initial Settings (Setup)	Shift-F1, 5
Insert	Ins
Insert, Forced	Home, Home, Ins
Italics	Ctrl-F8, 2, 4
Justification	Shift-F8, 1, 3
Kerning	Shift-F8, 4, 6, 1
Keyboard Layout	Shift-F1, 6
Language	Shift-F8, 4, 4
Large Print	Ctrl-F8, 1, 5
Line	
Draw	Ctrl-F3, 2
Format	Shift-F8, 1
Height	Shift-F8, 1, 4
Numbering	Shift-F8, 1, 5
Spacing	Shift-F8, 1, 6
List	
Define	Alt-F5, 5, 2
Mark (Block on)	Alt-F5, 2
List Files	F5, ↵
Location of Auxiliary Files	Shift-F1, 7
Look	F5, ↵, 6
Macro	Alt-F10
Macro Define	Ctrl-F10
←Margin Release	Shift-Tab
Margins	
Left/Right	Shift-F8, 1, 7
Top/Bottom	Shift-F8, 2,5
Mark Text	Alt-F5
Master Document	
Condense	Alt-F5, 6, 4
Expand	Alt-F5, 6, 3
Subdocument	Alt-F5, 2
Math/Columns	Alt-F7
Menu Letter Display	Shift-F1, 3, 7
Merge	Ctrl-F9, 1
Codes	Shift-F9
Move	Ctrl-F4
Block (Block on)	Ctrl-F4, 1
Page	Ctrl-F4, 3
Paragraph	Ctrl-F4, 2
Rectangle (Block on)	Ctrl-F4, 3
Rename (List Files)	F5, ↵, 3
Sentence	Ctrl-F4, 1
Tabular Column (Block on)	Ctrl-F4, 2

^N (Next Record)	Shift-F9, N
Name Search (List Files)	F5, ↵, N
New Page Number	Shift-F8, 2, 6
Normal Text (Turn Off Attributes)	Ctrl-F8, 3
Number of Copies	Shift-F7, N
^O (Display Message)	Shift-F9, 0
Other Directory	F5, ↵, 7
Outline	Shift-F5, 4
Outline (Attribute)	Ctrl-F8, 2, 5
Overstrike	Shift-F8, 4, 5
^P (Primary File)	Shift-F9, P
Page Format	Shift-F8, 2
Page Numbering	Shift-F8, 2, 7
Paragraph Number	Shift-F5, 5
Paragraph Numbering Definition	Shift-F5, 6
Paper Size/Type	Shift-F8, 2, 8
Password	Ctrl-F5, 2
Print	Shift-F7
Block (Block on)	Shift-F7, Y
Color	Ctrl-F8, 5
Full Document	Shift-F7, 1
List Files	F5, ↵, 4
Page	Shift-F7, 2
Printer	
Command	Shift-F8, 4, 6, 2
Settings	Shift-F7, S, 3
^Q (Stop Merge)	Shift-F9, Q
^R (End of Field)	Shift-F9, R
Redline	Ctrl-F8, 2, 8
Redline Method	Shift-F8, 3, 3
Remove Redline/Strikeout	Alt-F5, 6, 1
Repeat Value	Esc
Replace	Alt-F2
Replace, Extended	Home, Alt-F2
Retrieve	
Block (Move)	Ctrl-F4, 4, 1
Document	Shift-F10
List Files	F5, ↵, 1
Rectangle (Move)	Ctrl-F4, 4, 3
Tabular Column (Move)	Ctrl-F4, 4, 2
Reveal Codes	Alt-F3 or F11
Rewrite	Ctrl-F3, 0
Rush Print Job	Shift-F7, 4, 2
^S (Secondary File)	Shift-F9, S
Save	F10
Screen	Ctrl-F3
→Search	F2
→Search, Extended	Home, F2

←Search	Shift-F2
←Search, Extended	Home, Shift-F2
Select Printer	Shift-F7, S
Setup	Shift-F1
Shadow	Ctrl-F8, 2, 6
Shell	Ctrl-F1
Side-by-Side Column Display	Shift-F1, 3, 8
Size Attribute	Ctrl-F8, 1
Small Caps	Ctrl-F8, 2, 7
Small Print	Ctrl-F8, 1, 4
Sort	Ctrl-F9, 2
Spell	Ctrl-F2
Split Screen	Ctrl-F3, 1
Stop Printing	Shift-F7, 4, 5
Strikeout	Ctrl-F8, 2, 9
Style	Alt-F8
Subscript	Ctrl-F8, 1, 2
Superscript	Ctrl-F8, 1, 1
Suppress (Page Format)	Shift-F8, 2, 9
Switch	Shift-F3
^T (Send to Printer)	Shift-F9, T
Tab Align	Ctrl-F6
Tab Set	Shift-F8, 1, 8
Table (Graphics)	Alt-F9, 2
Table of Authorities	
Define	Alt-F5, 5, 4
Edit Full Form	Alt-F5, 5, 5
Full Form (Block on)	Alt-F5, 4
Short Form	Alt-F5, 4
Table of Contents	
Define	Alt-F5, 5, 1
Mark (Block on)	Alt-F5, 1
Text Box (Graphics)	Alt-F9, 3
Text In (List Files)	F5, ↵, 5
In/Out	Ctrl-F5
Text Quality	Shift-F7, T
Thesaurus	Alt-F1
Thousand's Separator	Shift-F8, 4, 3
Type Through	Shift-F7, 5
Typeover	Ins
Typeover, Forced	Home, Ins
^U (Rewrite Screen)	Shift-F9, U
Undelete	F1
Underline	F8 or Ctrl-F8, 2, 2
Underline Spaces/Tabs	Shift-F8, 4, 7
Units of Measure	Shift-F1, 8
User-Defined Box (Graphics)	Alt-F9, 4
^V (Insert Merge Code)	Shift-F9, V
Vertical Line (Graphics)	Alt-F9, 5, 2

Very Large Print	Ctrl-F8, 1, 6
View Document	Shift-F7, 6
Widow/Orphan Protection	Shift-F8, 1, 9
Window	Ctrl-F3, 1
Word/Letter Spacing	Shift-F8, 4, 6, 3
Word Search	F5, ↵, 9
Word Spacing Justification Limits	Shift-F8, 4, 6, 4
WordPerfect 4.2 Format	Ctrl-F5, 4

Cursor Control

Beginning of Document	Home, Home, ↑
Beginning of Line (Before Codes)	Home, Home, Home, ←
Beginning of Line (Before Text)	Home, Home, ←
Character Left	←
Character Right	→
End of Document	Home, Home, ↓
End of Line	Home, Home, → or End
Go To	Ctrl-Home
Line Down	↑
Line Up	↓
Page Down	PgDn
Page Up	PgUp
Screen Down	Home, ↓ or + (Num Pad)
Screen Left	Home, ←
Screen Right	Home, →
Screen Up	Home, ↑ or − (Num Pad)
Word Left	Ctrl-←
Word Right	Ctrl-→

A–7
WORDPERFECT 4.2 COMMAND SUMMARY

Feature	Keystrokes
Advance Line	Shift-F1
Advance Up/Down	Shift-F1
Alignment Character	Shift-F8
Append Block (Block on)	Ctrl-F4
Auto Hyphenation	Shift-F8, 5
Auto Rewrite	Ctrl-F3
Backspace	⬅
Binding Width	Shift-F7, 3
Block	Alt-F4
Block, Cut/Copy (Block on)	Ctrl-F4
Block Protect (Block on)	Alt-F8
Bold	F6
Cancel	F1
Cancel Hyphenation	F1
Cancel Print Job	Shift-F7, 4

Case Conversion (Block on)	Shift-F3
Center	Shift-F6
Center Page Top to Bottom	Alt-F8
Change Directory	F5, Return
Change Print Options	Shift-F7
Colors	Ctrl-F3
Column, Cut/Copy (Block on)	Ctrl-F4
Column, Text	Alt-F7
Column Display	Alt-F7
Concordance	Alt-F5, 6, 5
Conditional End of Page	Alt-F8
Copy	F5, Return
Create Directory	F5, =
Ctrl/Alt Key Mapping	Ctrl-F3
Dash	Home, —, —
Date	Shift-F5
Delete	Del
Delete (List Files)	F5, Return
Delete Directory (List Files)	F5, Return
Delete to End of Line (EOL)	Ctrl-End
Delete to End of Page (EOP)	Ctrl-PgDn
Delete to Left Word Boundary	Home, ←
Delete to Right Word Boundary	Home, Del
Delete Word	Ctrl-←
Display All Print Jobs	Shift-F7
Display Printers and Fonts	Shift-F7
Document Comments	Ctrl-F5
Document Conversion	Ctrl-F5
Document Summary	Ctrl-F5
DOS Text File	Ctrl-F5
Endnote	Ctrl-F7
Enter (or Return)	Enter
Escape	Esc
Exit	F7
Flush Right	Alt-F6
Font	Ctrl-F8
Footnotes	Ctrl-F7
Full Text (Print)	Shift-F7
Generate	Alt-F5, 6
"Go" (Resume Printing)	Shift-F7, 4
Go to DOS	Ctrl-F1
Hard Page	Ctrl-Enter
Hard Return	Enter
Hard Space	Home, Spacebar
Headers or Footers	Alt-F8
Help	F3
Home	Home
Hyphen	-

Hyphenation On/Off	Shift-F8, 5
H-Zone	Shift-F8, 5
→Indent	F4
→Indent←	Shift-F4
Index	Alt-F5
Insert Printer Command	Ctrl-F8
Justification On/Off	Ctrl-F8
Line Draw	Ctrl-F3
Line Format	Shift-F8
Line Numbering	Ctrl-F8
Lines Per Inch	Ctrl-F8
List (Block on)	Alt-F5
List Files	F5, Enter
Locked Documents	Ctrl-F5
Look	F5, Enter
Macro	Alt-F10
Macro Def	Ctrl-F10
◀Margin Release	Shift-Tab
Margins	Shift-F8
Mark Text	Alt-F5
Math	Alt-F7
Merge	Ctrl-F9
Merge Codes	Alt-F9
Merge E	Shift-F9
Merge R	F9
Minus Sign	Home, =
Move	Ctrl-F4
Name Search	F5, Enter
New Number (Footnote)	Ctrl-F7
New Page Number	Alt-F8
Number of Copies	Shift-F7, 3
Outline	Alt-F5
Overstrike	Shift-F1
Page (Print)	Shift-F7
Page Format	Alt-F8
Page Length	Alt-F8
Page Number Column Positions	Alt-F8
Page Number Position	Alt-F8
Paragraph Number	Alt-F5
Pitch	Ctrl-F8
Preview a Document	Shift-F7
Print	Shift-F7
Print (List Files)	F5, Enter
Print a Document	Shift-F7, 4
Print Block (Block on)	Shift-F7
Print Format	Ctrl-F8

Printer Control	Shift-F7
Printer Number	Shift-F7, 3
Proportional Spacing	Ctrl-F8, 1
Rectangle, Cut/Copy (Block on)	Ctrl-F4
Redline	Alt-F5
Remove	Alt-F5, 6
Rename	F5, Enter
Replace	Alt-F2
Replace, Extended	Home, Alt-F2
Retrieve	Shift-F10
Retrieve (List Files)	F5, Enter
Retrieve Column (Move)	Ctrl-F4
Retrieve Rectangle (Move)	Ctrl-F4
Retrieve Text (Move)	Ctrl-F4
Reveal Codes	Alt-F3
Rewrite	Ctrl-F3, Ctrl-F3
Rush Print Job	Shift-F7, 4
Save	F10
Screen	Ctrl-F3
>Search	F2
>Search, Extended	Home, F2
<Search	Shift-F2
<Search, Extended	Home, Shift-F2
Select Print Options	Shift-F7, 4
Select Printers	Shift-F7, 4
Sheet Feeder Bin Number	Ctrl-F8
Shell	Ctrl-F1
Short Form Marking	Alt-F5
Soft Hyphen	Ctrl=
Sort	Ctrl-F9
Sorting Sequences	Ctrl-F9
Spacing	Shift-F8
Spell	Ctrl-F2
Split Screen	Ctrl-F3, 1
Stop Printing	Shift-F7, 4
Strikeout (Block on)	Alt-F5
Super/Subscript	Shift-F1
Suppress Page Format	Alt-F8
Switch	Shift-F3
Tab	Tab
Tab Align	Ctrl-F6
Tab Ruler	Ctrl-F3, 1
Tab Set	Shift-F8
Table of Authorities (Block on)	Alt-F5
Table of Contents (Block on)	Alt-F5
Text In (List Files)	F5, Enter
Text In/Out	Ctrl-F5
Text Lines	Alt-F8, 4
Thesaurus	Alt-F1
Time	Shift-F5, 2

Top Margin	Alt-F8
Typeover	Ins
Type Thru	Shift-F7
Undelete	F1
Underline	F8
Underline Style	Ctrl-F8
Widow/Orphan	Alt-F8
Window	Ctrl-F3
Word Count	Ctrl-F2
Word Search	F5, Enter

A–8
COMMAND SUMMARY BY SPECIAL KEYS

Function Keys: WordPerfect 4.2

Key	Function
F1	Cancel, Cancel Hyphenation, Undelete
F2	Search
F3	To access On-Line Help
F4	Indent
F5	Retrieve, Delete, Rename, Print, Text In, Look, Change Directory, Copy, and Word Search
F6	Bold
F7	Exit
F8	Underline
F9	Merge R (to mark the end of a record in merge printing)
F10	Save

Alt and Function Keys: WordPerfect 4.2

Key	Function
Alt-F1	Thesaurus
Alt-F2	Replace
Alt-F3	Reveal Codes
Alt-F4	Turns Block feature on
Alt-F5	Table of Contents (Block on), Outline, Strike Out (Block on), Table of Authorities Index, List (Block on), Mark Redline, Short Form Marking
Alt-F5, 6	Generate Tables and Index, Remove All Redline Markings, Define Table of Contents
Alt-F5, 6, 5	Concordance Filename (includes all the phrases you want in the index)
Alt-F6	Flush Right
Alt-F7	Columns, Text, Columns Display, Math
Alt-F8	Paragraph Number, Suppress Page Format, Block Protect (Block on), Center Page Top to Bottom,

	Conditional End of Page, Headers or Footers, New Page Numbers, Page Format, Page Length, Page Number, Column Positions, Page Number Position, Top Margin, Widow/Orphan (A "widow" is the first line of a paragraph that is the last line on a page. An "orphan" is the last line of a paragraph that is the first line on a page.)
Alt-F8, 4	Text Lines
Alt-F9	Merge Codes
Alt-F10	To invoke a macro

Ctrl and Function Keys: WordPerfect 4.2

Key	Function
Ctrl-F1	Go to DOS
Ctrl-F2	Spell Check, Word Count
Ctrl-F3	Auto Rewrite, Colors, Line Draw, Screen, Window
Ctrl-F3, 1	Split Screen, Tab Ruler
Ctrl-F3, Ctrl-F3	Rewrite
Ctrl-F4	Append Block (Block on), Block, Cut/Copy, Move Rectangle, Cut/Copy (Block on), Retrieve Column (Move), Retrieve Rectangle (Move), Retrieve Text (Move)
Ctrl-F5	Document Conversion Commands, Document Summary, DOS Text File, Locked Documents, Text In/Out
Ctrl-F6	Tab Align
Ctrl-F7	Endnote, Footnote, New Number (Footnote),
Ctrl-F8	Font, Insert Printer Command, Justification On/Off, Line Numbering, Lines Per Inch, Pitch, Print Format, Sheet Feeder Bin Number, Underline Style
Ctrl-F8, 1	Proportional Spacing
Ctrl-F9	Merge, Sort
Ctrl-F10	Macro Definition
Ctrl-End	Delete to End of Line (EOL)
Ctrl-End	Delete to End of Page (EOP)
Ctrl-Backspace	Delete Word
Ctrl-Enter	Hard Page Break

Shift and Function Keys: WordPerfect 4.2

Key	Function
Shift-F1	Advance Line or Up/Down, Overstrike
Shift-F2	Search
Shift-F3	Case Conversion (Block on), Switch
Shift-F4	Right/Left Indent
Shift-F5	Date
Shift-F5, 2	Time
Shift-F6	Center

Shift-F7	Print Block (Block on), Printer Control, Full Text Print, Page Print, Preview of a Document, Change Print Options, Display All Print Jobs, Display Printers and Fonts, Type Thru
Shift-F7, 3	Binding Width, Number of Copies, Printer Number
Shift-F7, 4	Cancel Print Job, "Go" (Resume Printing), Print a Document, Rush Print Job, Select Print Options, Select Printers, Stop Printing
Shift-F8	Alignment Character, Line Format, Margins, Spacing, Tab Set
Shift-F8, 5	Auto Hyphenation, Hyphenation On/Off, H-Zone
Shift-F9	Merge E
Shift-F10	Retrieve a File

Editing and Arrow Keys: WordPerfect 4.2

Key	Function
Backspace	Deletes character to left of cursor
Ctrl-Home	Go To
Ctrl-left arrow	Word Left
Ctrl-right arrow	Word Right
Del	Deletes character at cursor
Esc	Cancels the action or repeat
Home-Del	Deletes to right word boundary
Home-left arrow	Screen Left
Home-right arrow	Screen Right
+ or Home and down arrow	Screen Down
− or Home, up arrow	Screen Up
PgDn	Page Down
PgUp	Page Up
Home-Home-up arrow	Beginning of text
Home-Home-down arrow	End of text
Home-Home-left arrow	Beginning of line (text)
Home-Home-Home-left arrow	Beginning of line (Codes)
Home-Home-right arrow	End of line
Down arrow	Moves the cursor down one line
Left arrow	Moves the cursor to the left by one position
Right arrow	Moves the cursor to the right by one position
Up arrow	Moves the cursor up one line

A–9
ANSWERS TO SELECTED REVIEW QUESTIONS

Chapter 1

2. Disk drive and keyboard.

6. Floppy and hard disks.

12. It varies. It starts at 256 or 512.

16. Keep it in a dust-free environment. Protect it against excessive heat and humidity. Provide a constant electrical current.

21. Every application program provides an editing feature so you can edit your mistakes. Or, in the worst case, you can retype your mistakes.

26. Priority of operations or precedence of operations refers to the order in which a computer handles calculations. The order is as follows:

- Expressions inside parentheses have the highest priority
- Exponentiation (raising to power) has the next highest priority
- Multiplication and division have the third highest priority
- Addition and subtraction have the fourth highest priority
- When there are two or more operations with the same priority, operations proceed from left to right

Chapter 3

3. Word processor, speller, thesaurus, merge, and advanced features.

8. Press F3 function key.

16. Insert is the default option. This means that when you type new text, the existing text is moved to the right. In "typeover" mode, you type over the existing character(s).

19. To save and exit use F7. To save and stay in the document, use F10.

21. Use Shift-PrtSc to print one screen at a time, or use Shift-F7 to enter the Print menu.

27. No. You have to save your work yourself. However, WordPerfect includes an automatic back-up feature that must be specified during the installation.

Chapter 4

1. Press F6.

5. Move the cursor to the specified text, and then check the number after Pos. If your text is underlined, this number is underlined. You can also reveal the formatting codes by pressing Alt-F3.

9. The Case Conversion command converts uppercase characters to lowercase and vice versa. Shift-F3. Yes.

11. Press Ctrl-F2. You must have the spell-check disk in one of your floppy drives or on your hard disk.

15. Press Alt-F1. You must have the thesaurus disk on your hard disk or in one of your floppy drives.

Chapter 5

3. No.

6. Press Alt-F3.

11. Press Shift-F3.

15. Press Ctrl-End.

24. The Cut command is used to transfer text from one location to another location.
26. Yes. Press F1. You will be able to restore the last three deletions.

Chapter 6

4. Press Ctrl-Enter. Press Del to remove it.
6. You have some flexibility: top center, bottom center, and so forth.
8. No.
14. They perform different tasks. For example, to mark the end of a field or a record, or to send output to the printer, and so on. See table 6–1.
17. Press Ctrl-F9 and select option 1.

Chapter 7

2. A footnote appears on the same page as its reference. Endnotes appear at the end of a document.
5. Press F7.
10. Press Ctrl-F8.
12. Press F7.
15. There are 9 sorting keys.
18. Press Ctrl-F9.

Chapter 8

4. Press Shift-F5.
8. A macro is a collection of keystrokes designed to perform a specific task.
12. Press Ctrl-F10.
21. Press Alt-F7.
23. It is non-numeric.

Index